You Mean, There's RACE in My Sports?

The Complete Guide for Understanding
Race & Sports in Mainstream Media

FREDERICK GOODING, JR.

On the Reelz
PRESS

This title is published by On the Reelz Press in association with The Race Doctor, Inc.
P.O. Box 6473, Silver Spring, Maryland, 20906, USA.

On the Reelz Press, and the On the Reelz Press logo are trademarks of
On the Reelz Press, Inc. The Race Doctor, and The Race Doctor logo
are trademarks of The Race Doctor, Inc.
www.theracedoc.com

ISBN: 978-0-9778048-6-3
Printed in the United States of America.

On the Reelz Press books may be purchased for educational, business, or personal use.
E-book editions are also available at www.amazon.com. For more information, contact
On the Reelz Press corporate/institutional sales department at http://otrpressinfo.
wixsite.com/website.

Special thanks to FG3.
and of courserous to our #1 fan . . .

DEDICATION

To those who remain "game"

TABLE OF CONTENTS

-ஓ ♮ ஏ-

NO HARM, NO FOUL?

Sports as Meritocracy; So What's the
Problem?

ET TU, LUDUS?

Sports are riveting. Sports are fun. Sports are exercise. Sports are unpredictable. Sports are enthralling. Sports are expressive. Sports are so many things to so many different people on this planet, that we must first recognize sports as a fundamental part of our larger human and specific cultural existence. This is not to say everyone engages sport at the same level in society, but a society without sport is rare indeed. Sports are many things, but surely, sports are not racist! [cue and insert scream here] For the love of all things righteous and true, no, not sports too! [wait for it...] "Say it ain't so Joe!"[1]

Well, the title of this book suggests that there is indeed a relationship. Our task is to parse out the nuances of how race intersects with sport for better or for worse as people play and watch sports — as these same people often are affected by larger societal issues. Many people personally enjoy sports for the thrill of the challenge — a championship season thus can represent how an individual or group of individuals maintained their focus, and withstood numerous challenges before emerging victorious at the end. This "gladiator mindset" fuels many who relish upon personal or intergroup competition.

Not to be presumptuous, but perhaps you the reader, currently are reading this book because you too, have a relationship with sports. As in, you played them, continue to play or patronize them. The question then remains, "are you game" to explore the relationship between race and sports? It may not be easy, but perhaps in our increasingly diverse world, such an inquiry is worthwhile indeed. For when we say "Race & Sports," not all of what we cover or discuss features virulent acts of vitriolic racism by only whites towards non-whites. Rather, we are interested in larger, systemic patterns and their societal implications.

FOR THE LOVE OF THE GAME

Sports are probably so popular because they have all the trappings of a melodramatic Italian opera or Greek play. There is tension, drama and of course, emotion. But what makes the emotion of sports unique is that it is tempered by a constant analytical presence. In other words, sports embody (literally) the key tensions between emotion and logic. There are those professionally affiliated with the world of sports that purely rely upon numbers, data and analysis to inform personnel moves, roster signings and game-time strategies. For instance, in Major League Baseball, "Sabermetrics," while not embraced by all, is employed by many (even have been spotlighted in the Hollywood production "Moneyball" starring Brad Pitt and Jonah Hill).[2] In the National Basketball Association, "Player Tracking" keeps precise track of statistics, such as how many assist opportunities a player has on a possession.[3] Yet, such data has no investment in the outcome.

But alas, we fickle sports fans indeed are invested in the outcome. Channel ABC sportscaster Jim McKay famously said it best for the program "ABC's Wide World of Sports" when he wisely observed that sports encompasses *the thrill of victory and the agony of defeat.*[4] It is well documented that whether during a championship match or a local, run of the mill league game, many a soul has been moved to tears, anger, joy and sadness — whether playing the game or merely spectating! It is quite common for people to personally connect with professional sports teams based upon purely regional or familial reasons ("My dad always took me to Phillies games," or "ever since I could remember, I was an Eagles fan like everyone else in my neighborhood"). Just think how often you have heard a sports fan refer to a privately held company as "my team." OK, great! But what does this tension between emotion and logic have to do with race?

MERITOCRACY RULES

For some, perhaps the two separate concepts of "race" and "sports" do not bear any instinctive connection since sports represent the last vestiges of true democracy in our country. Yes, the world of sport is one where meritocracy reigns supreme, all competitors are equal regardless of their race, and the best players are crowned based upon their "body of work." This philosophy of meritocracy, if anything, breaks down barriers between the races as all people are able to come together and cheer for the "spirit of the games." Athletes and teams earn what they get, plain and simple. Referees, umpires, standardized measurements and rules are all put in place and designed to prevent one opponent from obtaining an unfair advantage over another. Fair play encourages (but not ensures) equitable results.

With notions of fair play dominant in the societal psyche, explicit racism in or around contemporary American sports is difficult for many readers to grasp, for in contrast to other locations, America is doing pretty well. When looking at say, soccer in Europe or hockey in Canada, many documented cases exist of fans, players and owners making vile and racist comments openly and publicly.[5] While numerous efforts have been borne about to eradicate such behavior in the future (see Appendix A, "Box Score"), such behaviors have largely been written off as part of the "risk" or trade-off in playing professionally. One generally knows before joining a European soccer league team that this type of unpleasant behavior simply comes with the territory and that no direct personal offense should be taken.[6]

In America, on the whole, society has progressed to the point where direct and explicit public acts of racism at sporting events are infrequent and largely condemned. Whether it be Marge Schott,

Fuzzy Zoeller, John Rocker or Jimmy the Greek, any major faux pas associated with overt racism mostly occurred in the past.[7] American sports fans thereby operate largely off the implicit assumption that racism as we knew it, is extinct.

They are correct.

RACISM 2.0

Racism as we knew it is indeed extinct. It is currently downright unbecoming to appear in public as not having tolerance or to harbor disdain for diversity. Most of us are now more sensitive to the idea that people of different races should be respected in our new age. Yet, Racism 2.0 refers to the stubborn persistence of negative, disparaging narratives of old that are more refined and stylized and thus less obvious and overtly offensive in appearance. Present discrimination is much more subtle, suave and sophisticated in appearance and thereby more difficult to detect, let alone gain consensus upon.

Keys to the "New Game" of Racism 2.0	
Racism	Racism 2.0
• overt, obvious & offensive	• subtle, suave & sophisticated
Existing Tensions between Racism & Racism 2.0	
• more obvious vs. less offensive • historical basis vs. present oasis • similar messaging vs. different methodology • linear progress vs. literal progress	

The crux of this concept is that the mere absence of obvious markers of racism (e.g., hooded Ku Klux Klansmen burning crosses with nooses in their hands), does not mean that the *narratives* undergirding the obvious markers are any more absent. Such racially problematic thought patterns have been updated (i.e., 2.0) to increase capacity and efficiency while minimizing cost and waste, much like our quieter, faster and cleaner high-speed trains in contrast to the loud, lumbering and pollutive locomotives of old. While American society has made significant social improvements specifically around the topic of race over the years, current data suggest that there may still remain a smidgen of room for slight improvement.[8] Many Americans and several pockets of America still observe "poor habits" from the past – whether consciously or unconsciously – that perpetuate class, gender and racial discrimination amongst other Americans. Such discrimination is implied generally by statistical data, but seldom acknowledged directly amongst individuals who have been raised by their parents not to "see the color of another's skin" but to see "the content of one's character." Within these pages, we aim to tackle this very issue directly. There was indeed a time when America and its major professional sports were racist. It is now time to explore whether our present day sports are free from racism or whether under principles of Racism 2.0 the same game exists under a different name?

BOOK FORMAT

At On the Reelz Press, we believe the most precious resource of all is time, ergo time is always of the essence. Our specialty-crafted Modus Operandi or M.O. is to therefore get *2 tha Point* with *FullProof Analysis*, then step out the way before you *Just Add Water* to see your understanding grow.

2 tha Point

Since time is of the essence, we seek to unburden our readers with only 10 chapters of only 10 pages of content or less

FullProof

What makes our content virtually foolproof is that we are literally full of proof, as in, we provide at least ten (10) references or more for each chapter. This pragmatic approach underscores our strong preference for careful observation rather than careless opinion.

Just Add Water

Once our concepts are firmly rooted within the fertile landscape of your consciousness, you are free to add your own analysis and experiences to the foundational rubrics (e.g., Sportotypes) to test and see your understanding grow before your very eyes!

To allow for proper exposition of the relationship between Race & Sports, this book is divided into ten chapters of no more than ten pages of content apiece. Chapter One provides a brief historical contextualization of the relationship between Race and Sports; readers will better appreciate this relationship by having a reference point for the biggest American racial rivalry. Chapter Two then outlines the analytical rubric that serves as the anchor for this manuscript: the Sportotypes. Virtually all non-white athletes competing in major professional sports are framed in at least one of six consistent ways by mainstream media. The contours of these patterns are fleshed out in Chapters Three through Eight, each dedicated to one of the six Sportotypes. Chapter Nine focuses on the opposite side of the field, or coverage of white athletes by mainstream media to help round out our perspective. Chapter Ten then summarizes key points from the previous chapters and offers specific takeaways for readers still desirous for more information on the topic.

The Gameplan

Lastly, it is important to note that while the substantive content of this book is appropriate for academic purposes, in addition to being suitable for fans of all types, this book freely employs a "jocular style of writing" (get it?). In other words, while the thoughts and concepts contained herein are certainly complex, the phraseology is not riddled with academic jargon. Rather than preemptively apologize for this text not sounding "academic enough," if anything, the author is selectively employing the rules of artistic expression frequently and freely employed within the wide world of sports to more effectively communicate ideas. Thus, do no be alarmed over the occasional use of "slang" or "conventional sentence construction" for sometimes, the most formal tone does not always score points with the reader.

Yet, to be clear: this is not an all-inclusive text that will break down every sports trope or mainstream media example. Nor is this book an all-encompassing, exhaustive encyclopedia that includes every example about every athlete imaginable. Nor is this book conceived as an all out diss of your favorite sport simply because it does not meet criteria of consistent nationwide exposure. Nor is it an exhaustive or strained tribute to the Philadelphia Eagles that is unceasingly forced upon the reader. Instead, this manuscript is interested in fleshing out the relationship between Race & Sports and providing a foundational rubric for the reader to continue to build upon now that they have anchoring concepts to serve as a guide.

NO SWEAT

Do you wanna play a game?

The objective here is to start with a rebuttable presumption and then see after considering the evidence presented throughout the manuscript whether the rebuttable presumption can "go the distance," or ends up being "knocked out." No "split decisions" will be allowable. In the end, there must emerge a lone victor.

Rebuttable Presumption
"There is NO racism in American sport."
1. Sports are a meritocracy.
2. Due to emphasis on results and not "color," many non-white athletes have been able to achieve success.
3. Therefore, mainstream media objectively reports on those who perform well within the meritocracy, using logical statistics and results as a guide, thereby eliminating racism.

Many American citizens find the very suggestion of the very topic of racism problematic, especially in light of the fact that Barack Obama's historic 2008 election victory as President of the United States of America and the subsequent ushering in of a new "post-racial" society.[9] Thus, for a country that used to *enslave* black citizens to move to a point where it is able to *elect* black citizens to serve as the Chief Executive for one of the world's leading superpowers clearly symbolizes progress on some level. Continued debate and dialogue about the true level of progress will ensue within the pages of this manuscript as we must now prepare for game time; the battle of wits over old and new bodies of knowledge is now on!

The game is now afoot! We shall presently test this rebuttable presumption to determine whether this is true....

Keys to the Game

- *KNOW:* the definition of meritocracy

- All of our references located in Appendix A, "Box Score" employ the MLA style

- Being an honorable Philadelphia Eagles fan is not a prerequisite for reading, understanding and appreciating the material presented forthwith

- However, being an honorable Philadelphia Eagles fan is often referred to in certain circles as a "true measure of humanity"; thus while being an honorary Eagles fan whilst reading this text is not required, it is certainly recommended

THE PLAYING FIELD

Where Power & Control are the Goals

RECAPPING THE RACIAL RIVALRY

With respect to "Race and Sports," race is an open term that generally refers to Native Americans, Latino/Chicano Americans, Black Americans, Asian Americans, White Americans, among others in this text. However, in this country, "race" is often a euphemism that refers primarily to black and white relations based upon historical attention to this binary. Many racial groups have suffered discrimination in this country. However, the history between White Americans and Black Americans is particularly extensive, making the two groups historically inseparable in this country. It is difficult to tell the story of one without invoking the history of the other.

Without going into a painfully long historical lesson here, suffice to be said that early Americans' enslavement of African Americans and subsequent treatment of Native Americans while settling the "New World" under principles of Manifest Destiny made for some possible contradictions to fundamental democratic principles from the country's inception.[1] In the two centuries that followed after the country's founding, tensions behind building a strong and prosperous nation often conflicted with how other racial groups, such as Latino Americans in the southwest and Asian Americans in the west, were perceived as fitting into the American Dream.

Conversely, not all White Americans had an easy time settling in America and establishing prosperous lifestyles. The mass immigration movement of the early twentieth century demonstrated that many Irish, Jewish and Italian Americans were denigrated and separated by neighborhoods within the large urban metropolises (i.e., ghettos) and had a difficult time integrating into the mainstream. However, while not easy, many Whites or at least those who presented as White, had a *less difficult* time becoming successful. Why? Well, there were concrete and systemic social, legal and economic barriers institutionalized from the country's beginning that frustrated one's "pursuit of happiness" especially if one was African American or Black. Again, without indulging our nation's long and rich history on race relations, suffice to be said that Jim Crow segregationist laws, voting rights restrictions, convict leasing programs, redlining bank lending practices and unchecked violent vigilantism were just some of the barriers blocking blacks from "fair play" within the American Dream — most especially for southern Blacks until the mid-1950s — right around the time where many of our major sports leagues began to integrate.[2]

In other words, we would be "poor sports" indeed to have a contemporary conversation about sports, and not acknowledge this historical narrative, especially in light of the large influence black athletes have at the professional level. This is not to say that sports today are still operating in the ethos of enslavement, which was an extreme form of "unfair play," although authors like William C. Rhoden do make that case in *Forty Million Dollar Slaves*.[3] But rather, that today's sports climate was not created within a vacuum. How the past affects the present is part of the evolving dynamic narrative surrounding one of the biggest "racial rivalries" the country has ever seen.

We now know that the United States of America, home of the great democratic experiment, is in many ways a work in progress and thus did not always operate optimally when it came to its stated ideals of life, liberty and the pursuit of happiness. While numerous changes over time can be enumerated, our history is nonetheless replete with examples of many institutional barriers systematically erected to thwart Blacks (males in particular) from openly competing with Whites on the open market — both in society and especially in sport![4]

So, the next question is how does this racial rivalry, or racialized history between Whites and Blacks, affect the current playing field? Well, one can argue that despite the meritocratic nature of sports generally, that the game is nonetheless "rigged" when it specifically comes to race.

FAIR GAME?

Do you wanna play a game?

Have you ever been to a carnival?

If you have, then you know first hand about the numerous experiences available that add up to a good time. First, there are the rides. Then, there is the food — food is absolutely instrumental in such an experience. What else? Why, for many of us, the carnival games are an additional source of welcomed merriment!

Do you wanna play a carnival game?

The oversized stuffed creations gently sway from their perches on high and ever so softly, silently mock us and dare us into winning them. For the true challenge of the carnival game is that you indeed have to emerge victorious. While many may want such a prize, only those brave enough to compete for it will earn the burden of schlepping it around the park for the rest of afternoon and evening, a small cross to bear that connotes more respect and admiration than it does shame from onlooking bystanders. So participating in the rides is easy; just simply wait in line. Obtaining food is equally simple — simply decide what you want and wait in line as well.

Now, for the carnival games, much more thought and strategy is required. For we all know from the outset that while the task looks easy, it may be anything but. After all, a quick mental inventory may reveal that out of hundreds, you actually saw only two to three people walking around with one of those stuffed cartoon characters big enough to fill your bathtub if ripped open and allowed to bleed its stuffing out.

Assuming that these stuffed monstrosities cost money, and that in our capitalistic society, most entities, including carnival game owners, seek to obtain a profit from their endeavors, then, it follows that carnival games are not in the business of just giving away these large stuffed entities. They *need you to fail* more times than you succeed; otherwise, they would not be in business. As unpleasant as that may sound, it is worthy of restating so that we are all clear. Carnival games succeed in business when you fail.

A business that is designed around failure must be delicate about going about its business, after all, no one wants to be a sucker and few people like to willingly part with their money — especially if they do not have much to begin with. So it is not without coincidence that you have many in the carnival game industry using subtle tips and tricks to keep the public interested in playing, while they are not themselves completely interested in paying. In other words, *carnival game syndrome* is the axiom that *while possible, it is not plausible* to win the attendant scenario. Take the balloon darts game for instance. Did you know that they often use older balloons so that the rubber is tougher to penetrate for the dull darts they provide you?[5] Or that for the milk jug toss, the jugs at the bottom are weighted with lead?[6] Or that for the remote-controlled grappling arm, that the arm strength is programmed to be weaker nine times out of ten?[7]

Thus, what if the American Dream was a game, and it too was rigged? Meaning, that it was *possible* for blacks and other minorities to "win," but that it was not *plausible* en masse? For the simplistic sake of argument and example, if we were to hypothetically label those of the white race as being on Team White and those of African American descent as being on Team Black, historically, members of Team White have accumulated "more points" towards the American Dream, if one considers education, family wealth, income, property acquisition, representation in government as reasonable indicators.[8]

Just as there will always be one or two winners out of hundreds walking around with a large carnival prize, such a sampling is not indicative of how fair or unfair the opportunity to win the prize truly was. When it comes to established institutions such as education, politics, economics and the like, in this country these realms have been traditionally dominated by Team White. While technically open to competition from anyone, it is unlikely that Team White will completely relinquish their grip or dynasty over these institutions any time soon. And much like with "deflategate" and the New England Patriots, there has been speculation about whether all of Team White's victories have been achieved in the spirit of "fair play."[9] Some might even attribute some of these competitive discrepancies to racism.

TRIPLE TEAMING THE UNHOLY TRINITY

Racism is irrational and illogical. Fine. Now that we have gotten that kernel of truth out of the way, the fact remains that many rational people must devise rational responses to racism, ergo this manuscript. From the country's inception, many early White Americans have had an obsession or preoccupation with race when "moving" Native Americans out of the way in the name of Manifest Destiny and utilizing the "necessary evil" of enslavement as the most efficient means of developing this "New World."

What we now know to be morally reprehensible was both legal and commonplace. What we must interrogate is whether we should not judge early settlers too harshly as times have changed and the men and women of past era were merely "products of their time," or whether condemnation is in order because they knew in their hearts that what they were wrong back then too?

At any rate, while not all Whites held people hostage as slaves,[10] much of America was still a slave society (just like all citizens presently do not own cars, but much of our society and daily life is significantly affected by them). Further, this slave society could not have existed for more than two centuries unless many significant actors devised working rationales. These rationales worked together to maintain a system that would normally wilt under critical scrutiny. However, there are three irrefutable historical themes that operated as an "intellectual shorthand" and provided white members of the slave society with just enough rationale to combat the rational argument against slavery (as espoused in the Declaration of Independence):

Romantic Racialism

Romantic Racialism was a very influential 19th century theme that propagated the narrative that blacks were actually *superior* to whites, but only within limited, subjugated contexts. Thus, black slaves were lauded for their physical stature and skill, but only in relation to how their production increased profits for the plantation owner. Blacks were seen as physically gifted and were also admired for their ability to sing, dance and praise the Lord despite their oppressed existence. A false sense of racial comity developed where many whites were convinced that they actually liked and appreciated blacks, but it was not a deep abiding love or respect. At an early stage, blacks were primarily valued for their performances only.[11] The sports industry is one of the few industries where based upon rules of meritocracy, whites have been forced to acknowledge exceptional black performances, or "superiority."

Femininity

Femininity focused on the enslaved black's relationship with his white captor. The height of fantasy was for whites to go to bed guilt free at night, knowing that the enslaved blacks who worked at their plantation did so because they somehow enjoyed it or wanted to. This fictive narrative stems from the general anthromorphization of races to genders, and the white race was seen as a "masculine" race due to its ability to build and design whereas the black race was seen as "feminine," or more docile and better suited for servile positions — whether male or female.[12] Hence, this narrative fooled many a white plantation owner into believing that the enslaved present simply had no other lot in life. Harriet Beecher Stowe's titular character, Uncle Tom from *Uncle Tom's Cabin*, embodied this image of an older, non-threatening, devoutly religious and fiercely devoted slave who was willingly sacrificed everything for his master. It is no coincidence a black character molded in femininity took firm hold inside the mainstream consciousness given the political climate of the time.[13]

Negrophobia

Negrophobia developed later in the Enslavement Era and was a preemptive narrative used to justify and defend whites against threatening blacks. The only issue here is that such justifications often required great leaps of logic of which were ultimately immaterial to the user. Mostly whites enslaved blacks against their will. Many blacks resisted, rebelled or at least, thought about doing so. Many whites placed themselves in the shoes of the enslaved and thought about the anger and outrage they would feel if placed in such a position. Many whites then feared the "backlash" they might receive from the enslaved if freedom was ever obtained for all. Thus, any slight perception of black anger was to be immediately distrusted as dangerous and had to be quelled and subdued — forcefully if need be.

Negrophobia later expanded to include the unexplained, fiery hate that many whites openly exhibited towards blacks. For instance, members of vigilante groups such as the Ku Klux Klan often "cited" fears of miscegenation, rape and joblessness for whites if blacks were allowed to run amok unchecked, thereby requiring the need to keep the "negro in his place."[14] This negrophobia fueled many of our country's lynchings and other terrorist acts of violence against members of the black community and their allies.[15] Yet, very seldom have sustained, systemic mass attacks of whites against blacks been historically documented as a "justified" defense in response to sustained, systemic mass attacks of blacks upon whites. In most cases, the impetus behind tensions underlying this racial rivalry was sparked by Team White playing on the offensive side of the ball. *NOTE*: the exceptional cases of Nat Turner and Denmark Vesey's separate uprisings were neutralized and quashed in relatively short order.

While defeatist principles of the Unholy Trinity may apply to any and all persons, this country has an established history of employing them consistently and explicitly against Blacks. As a result, many Blacks and their continued competition for life, liberty and the pursuit of happiness have consequently become the "touchstone of the modern democratic idea...and puts our democracy to the proof and reveals the falsity of it."[16]

BALL IS LIFE

Ergo, the beauty and appeal of sport.

Perhaps, just perhaps, as a means to counter against the destructive forces of the Unholy Trinity, many have taken to sport as a conscious/ subconscious declaration of their humanity. There are three "defenses," or compelling considerations for why sports (especially basketball and football) contain sustained appeal and success for Black athletes as evidenced by current participation rates:

Consistency

In keeping with the theme that sports are the last dominion of "fair play" based upon their underlying ethos of meritocracy, sports "make sense" to a lot of people of color for whereas it is difficult to understand or explain the seemingly inconsistent application of "the rules" in civil society, in sport, there is more consistency. The basketball rims in China are ten feet tall, the same height as they are in Australia and America or anywhere else in the world where "basketball" is played. The rules of sport create a universal standard for judgment.

Competition

Based upon the solid foundation of consistency, vigorous competition can exist. Participants can receive instantaneous feedback about their "value" to their team or the sport based upon results. As opposed to the more fluid and fungible social measures in society, it is clear at the end of a game who scored the most points, goals, baskets, yards, touchdowns, or what have you. When considering Jim Crow segregation, for instance, society might dictate where one can use the restroom or which bench to sit upon, but in sport, no one else besides the shooter can dictate if the ball will or will not go through the hoop if it is shot accurately and correctly. Similarly, the smaller feedback loop associated with one's own body fuels competitive juices whereby the pushups and sit-up exercises performed today will make for a stronger body tomorrow (if done consistently and with vigor, that is) as opposed to the more abstract concept of "working hard" on the job where a Horatio Alger, "Bound to Rise" trajectory is less certain.[17]

Catharsis

For many Blacks especially, when raised in lower income environments where it appears that no amount of study in school will change completely the sense of hopelessness and dread seemingly innate to the surrounding community,[18] sports become a cathartic outlet because the athlete is in control of their life for once.

Unlike the mind-numbing propositions whereby even after working for an advanced education, many individuals are still not protected from unemployment,[19] through sport, there is a greater sense of satisfaction of reaping a direct investment from one's labors. This gratification is heightened by the belief that the future can also be more readily influenced by one's specific actions in competition.

Sports also create space for liberated expression and provide tangible focal points for the constructive release of internal energy. Football and basketball especially allow for "me against the world" dynamics that may parallel an athlete's real life off the playing surface. Consider the running back or wide receiver in football whereby athletes must successfully out-maneuver, elude, out-run or in some cases, overrun multiple opponents for significant distances. Or how in basketball, the act of slam dunking is a public, definitive demonstration of one first defying gravity to "fly" in the air and then secondly defying the opponent by imposing one's will towards a goal. Period.

Such acts are often accompanied by immediate validation from peers. Not to mention, such successful acts count as immediate progress towards personal and team goals of emerging victorious. For if we all love anything, we all love a *winner*. For some then, these games can be more than just a game. The direct gratification extracted from sport can be life changing, if not life itself.

Keys to the Game

- *KNOW:* the Unholy Trinity

- *KNOW:* the three "defenses" to the Unholy Trinity

INTRODUCING THE PLAYERS

Starting Lineups from the Media Guide

FINAL FOUR

If you love sports, then chances are that you appreciate the "spirit of the games" in whatever form it takes. So long as there is robust competition for points in a format that you can understand, then you are game. Alas, within this text, by way of transparency, most of the focus will be on two sports leagues in particular. In case you are wondering whether this is a "bait & switch" (to borrow a fishing term) scenario to use the all-encompassing title "Race & Sports," yet primarily concentrate on two sports, we shall presently explain.

In the spirit of competition, we focus our energy on those at the top. Numerous leagues and associations populate our sports landscape. But alas, there can only be one victor. We highlight the "Primary Sports" category since they enjoy maximum exposure and are structured and packaged to reach the greatest possible audience, thereby having the greatest potential for cultural impact and influence. For instance, field hockey fans number aplenty, but nationally televised games for a professional field hockey league spanning eight months do not.

Primary Sports	Secondary Sports	Tertiary Sports
ubiquitous year-round mainstream professional market	established professional & amateur market	limited professional market; mostly seasonal & amateur
• NFL (National Football League) • NBA (National Basketball Ass'n) • MLB (Major League Baseball) • NHL (National Hockey League) _NOTE_: The sports listed within these three columns are not exhaustive	• NCAA (DI basketball & football) • USTA (Tennis) • PGA (Golf) • MLS (Major League Soccer) • NASCAR (Car Racing) • WNBA (Women's National Basketball Ass'n)	• Volleyball • Surfing • Skiing • Ice Skating • Track & Field • Olympic Sports (Winter & Summer) • Drag Racing • Equestrian Riding • Softball • Lacrosse • Field hockey • Gymnastics • Fishing

In looking at the numbers, with revenue being an indicator of popularity and patronage, the National Football League is king. More appropriately, they are "king of the world" in that no other professional sports league on the planet outgrosses them. In fact, four of the top five earning professional sports leagues worldwide all are based in the United States of America. The English Premier Soccer League is third on the list, just in front of the NBA @ $5 billion in annual revenues for the same time period listed below.[1]

League	Annual Revenue (2013-14)	Season
NFL	$11.2B	16 games (September - February)
MLB	$9B	162 games (April - October)
NBA	$5B	82 games (October - June)
NHL	$3.6B	82 games (October - June)

Within this text, individual sports such as car racing, horse racing, tennis, track and field and golf will receive some mention, but not nearly as much based upon their lower levels of mainstream popularity as evidenced by revenues — a crude but necessary metric within our capitalistic society. While many of these other Secondary and Tertiary sports are extremely popular and take place around the year, coverage for these events is usually heightened for a specific event with less frequency (i.e., the Olympics, World Championships, World Cups, Opens, etc.). As the Primary Sports are more visible, examples from these leagues are more prominent and visible within mainstream media. Recall, Hollywood made a movie starring Kevin Costner entitled "Draft Day"[2] featuring the NFL — not Major League Soccer despite soccer's overwhelming worldwide popularity — likely as indication of what Hollywood sees as a more bankable product.

So we have four American Primary Sports that command our immediate attention — how do we whittle our list down to two?

INSIDE THE NUMBERS

Of the four American Primary Sports leagues, a racial lens reveals that two leagues in particular have a majority of Black players.[3]

League	% Black	Year of Integration
NFL	68.7%	1946
MLB	8.5%	1947
NBA	76.3%	1950
NHL	5%	1958

Hence, when we talk about "Race & Sports," most of the more visible tensions manifest within mainstream media implicate, involve or include black players who dominate in both performance and in population for two of the top four grossing leagues in the *world* — not bad for a demographic that is only 13% of America's total population.[4]

The working definition of "Race & Sports" offered in the foregoing paragraph may make for a rather limiting and narrow definition in light of the widening spectrum that is "sport" worldwide. Yet, the sheer volume of blacks within NFL and NBA have allowed for certain patterns of conduct to emerge within mainstream media over time. Such patterns are not as prodigious, prevalent or pronounced with Asian American players or Native American players that are sparsely represented within the top earning Primary Sports. This is not to say such members of such groups do not suffer from racism in sport. Our focus is simply upon the individuals within the sports that receive the most amounts of coverage, and consequently, scrutiny.

By way of quick example, consider NBA player LeBron James's "Decision" during the summer of 2012. If you follow basketball, you remember it well — this was when Mr. James decided to leave the franchise of his home state of Ohio, the Cleveland Cavaliers, and "take his talents to South Beach," to become a member of the Miami Heat.[5] The backlash and ensuing fallout was remarkable not just for its racial implications (of which we shall unpack later), but for how it dominated mainstream media news outlets at the time – and subsequently still receives reference. Yet, we are talking about one solitary NBA player during the offseason. This is an example of how the NBA is stronger within mainstream circles than say, the top earning NHL which would be hard pressed to generate weeks of continued coverage for a star who left the Vancouver Canucks for the Colorado Avalanche.

With respect to the larger conversation about "racism within sport," an ongoing debate must be fleshed out regarding the use of Native and Arab Americans as mascots for high school, collegiate and professional sports teams.[6] Additionally, MLB has 30% Latinos,[7] so many of the patterns seen for black players within the NBA and NFL are replicated for Latinos within MLB, where the overwhelming majority of the owners, fans, front office, sponsors and covering press are white. Suffice to be said, "majority white" is not inherently bad (ask my teeth), yet such disparity presents a social dynamic whereupon two different cultures may clash on public stages in public ways. Within this text, we explore this relationship between highly visible non-white athletes and the largely invisible white men who watch them.

Finally, given the contextualization of the "racial rivalry" between blacks and whites within America, the history between these two groups is documented, extensive and unique. Black athletes' achievements or *faux pas* covered by mainstream media cannot be separated from this history cleanly or convincingly in all instances. Thus, race is often a factor with such media coverage. The question then simply becomes: "Provided race is a factor, how much of a factor?"

WHITE DYNASTY

Despite having played the game "less time" than whites, with the likely exception of NHL, black players have liberally and literally colored the pages of Hall of Fame record books within the NFL, NBA and MLB. Yet, whites still dominate in sports within three key areas: Proprietorship, Patronage and Press.

Proprietorship

Of the 122 teams between the four Primary Sports, only four, or 3.2% boast nonwhite majority owners. Shahid Khan of Pakistani descent owns the NFL franchise Jacksonville Jaguars, Shanghai-born Charles Wang owns the NHL New York Islanders, Arturo "Arte" Moreno owns the MLB Los Angeles Angels of Anaheim and NBA great Michael Jordan owns the NBA Charlotte Hornets.[8]

League	% Nonwhite Ownership	% White Ownership
NFL	3.1%	97%
MLB	3.3%	100%
NBA	3.3%	97%
NHL	3.3%	100%

Despite the increasing number of nonwhite players who have cycled through and are looking for ways to still give back or stay connected to "the game," the overwhelming majority of front office administrators and staff on most professional teams are white. Coaching ranks are similarly dismal for diversity. The seemingly intractable problem of black head coaches never landing an opportunity to coach prompted the NFL to adopt a new policy entitled "The Rooney Rule," named after the late Pittsburgh Steelers owner who hired black coach Mike Tomlin as the franchise's third coach ever.[9] NCAA experiences similarly dismal disparities in non-white male coaches.[10]

Additionally, proprietorship is displayed through the majority white fan base that operates upon a "shareholder model," whereupon by investing heavily into the team via paraphernalia or season tickets, they now have the license and authority to either praise or criticize just as heavily. Just listen patiently to sports talk radio long enough and listen for the disgruntled fan to utter, "I pay his salary" in response to an underperforming or "misbehaving" athlete.

Patronage

Patronage manifests in two primary ways: attendance and sponsorship. For instance, attendance records indicate the following:[11]

League	% White Attendance	% Black Attendance
NFL	50>%?	@ 7.9%
MLB	30>%?	@ 6.1%
NBA	50>%?	@12.3%
NHL	50>%?	???

Hence, the term "the fans" is largely a euphemism to describe a majority white fan base. Further, attendance records call into question who exactly has time and leisure to attend a MLB game "businessman's special," or game that starts mid-afternoon during the work week?[12] Or who can attend all three games of a home stand series? Who purchases season/playoff tickets and/or inherits them? These are more delicate questions that may intersect along lines of class and race.

When considering the Brobdingnagian support of external partners necessary to maintain high revenues, what exactly do we mean by corporate sponsors? When we consider the income stream from the naming rights, advertisements at ballparks and arenas, television contracts and commercials, who exactly are these corporate sponsors?

Most of the corporate partners are companies established enough to provide millions of dollars annually without a guarantee of return. Many are Fortune 500 companies and virtually all are overwhelmingly white-owned.[13] How many major professional sports arenas or stadiums in America can you think of that feature the naming rights of a company owned (not just the CEO) by a nonwhite American?

To be clear, when it comes to naming rights, much is at stake. The money companies pay each year to be official sponsors — not including advertising and promotions is worth about $1.07 billion for the league and all of its teams, according to sponsorship consultancy IEG. The NFL is a coveted partner for mainstream brands since an average of 17.4 million people tune in during a regular season NFL game and the Super Bowl is the most watched show on the planet.[14]

Press

Sports media always has been and still is white male dominated:[15]

Profession	% White	% Black
Entire Staff	86%	7.6%
Columnists	84%	21.3%
Reporters	86.3%	7.7%
Editors	90.9%	5.7%

Given the obvious dynamic between white dominated sportswriters, black dominated entertainment sports (e.g., NBA & NFL), we must remain sensitive to the tensions between honest critiques of play versus historical criticism of players based upon problematic race-based narratives influenced by the Unholy Trinity. All athletes face pressure from fans and the media, but white athletes tend to benefit from an assets-based belief that the athlete can or will achieve as a person, whereas nonwhite athletes often suffer from a deficit-based approach that is often hypercritical and punitive of mistakes that should not be made.

For instance, consider the pairing of Derek Carr and Jameis Winston. Both gentlemen (as of Fall, 2015) were starting NFL quarterbacks. Both gentlemen were drafted in the first round of their respective drafts, with Carr going as the thirty-sixth pick in 2014 and with Winston as the first selection overall in 2015. Both also lost their first ever NFL games as starters. Both gentlemen received different media coverage. Carr "learned "he belonged on that big stage already at the start of his rookie season even if the end result wasn't quite what he hoped," while Winston was simply "inept."[16] Notwithstanding the emotion behind the baggage that Winston brought with him from Florida State,[17] in judging the two solely off their NFL debuts of one game apiece, one quarterback had an ominous start to his entire career while the other had one bad game, but hopefully would improve.

These differences in tone can be classified as forms of either *supportive* or *suppressive* pressure. We shall explore this tension at length through the Sportotypes.

Different Types of Pressure Athletes Face	
Supportive (usu. white athletes)	Suppressive (usu. nonwhite athletes)
• mistakes are contextualized • errors couched in encouragement • achievements celebrate personal qualities extending beyond sport	• mistakes criticized & overanalyzed • errors shrouded in derision • achievements celebrate physical qualities within world of sport

THE SPORTOTYPES

While historically documented with data and statistics, racism and racial discrimination is nonetheless an emotional topic for many. To ease with this difficulty, we will now introduce our "Starting Lineup" for this text, or our principal analytical rubric that will (hopefully) carry us logically to victory by the conclusion of this text. This rubric consists of six consistent athlete profile patterns seen in mainstream sports. In recognizing their consistency, we will provide a stable foundation with which to meaningfully analyze race without us appearing to randomly select examples just to prove a specific point.[18]

Many of us involved in sport understand that when two competitors do battle, it is often useful to have agreed upon *rules of engagement* and a means to enforce these rules. At the professional level, referees and umpires undergo extensive training over the course of years to be prepared to respond instantly to human movement, as it is human nature to gain a competitive advantage "within the rules" wherever possible. Hence, the *sportotypes* rubric will serve as our rules of engagement. Sportotypes are benign, but re-occurring media patterns for non-white sports figures that appear harmless on an individual basis, but nonetheless contribute to a message of marginalization in the aggregate. Referees, like rubrics, are not perfect and sometimes miss crucial, game-changing calls. Yet, these leagues invest considerable resources to ensure that while human nature and behavior in sport is not an exact science, maintaining the integrity of the game should be as consistent a process as possible. This rubric will allow us to do precisely the same in our discussion about race and sports.

The Sportotypes comprise two groups based upon traditional white perspectives of *fear* and *fascination* of the black body, based upon the Unholy Trinity of race relations briefly outlined in Chapter 1. The fear is fueled by irrational projections of negrophobia whereas the fascination is nurtured by enduring ideas of romantic racialism and femininity. Hence, the Sportotypes are organized as follows:

Menace to Society	Diva	Intellectually Suspect	Model Citizen	Comic Relief	Buck
FEAR			FASCINATION		
Negrophobia	Femininity	Rom. Racialism	Negrophobia	Femininity	Rom. Racialism

Other women and men of color fit within these six total classifications, but it is imperative to underscore the historical origins of such groupings. In America, not only has the mainstream constantly and generally been fixated on race since the country's inception,[15] but the black body and power and control of it specifically has been at target. Whether it was Venus Hottentot, Ota Benga or Henrietta Lacks, or using faulty IQ testing to justify faulty racialized educational policies, the black body and its brain have been the source of constant prodding and poking, via constant vacillation between fear and fascination by white gazers.[19]

In each of the six subsequent chapters profiling Sportotypes, at least ten examples are provided to illustrate the contours of how each analytical concept works. The included examples are not all encompassing, representative or definitive — they are just a brief list of excellent examples to which you will undoubtedly add more (or *Just Add Water*). To show how ubiquitous the Sportotypes are, each example set will start with the well-known, non-NBA/NFL athlete Tiger Woods. Mr. Woods is not only famous for winning fourteen different golf "major" tournaments, but he is also famous for having perhaps just as many extra-marital affairs come to light in the aftermath of a Thanksgiving 2009 domestic incident (which will for now and hereafter will be referred to as "the incident").[20] Since Mr. Woods is so iconic, he serves as an excellent reference point for readers to see the familiar in new ways through the Sportotypes while simultaneously illustrating how an athlete can exhibit characteristics of more than one Sportotype.

PUT ME IN, COACH!

Good news, bad news! Let's start with the bad news first. The bad news is that with all of the examples provided throughout the subsequent pages, not all examples are likely to feature athletes with whom you may be readily familiar. Many are "older" athletes or may be "non-name brand" athletes with shorter careers within the top Primary Sports. And uh, that might be precisely the point!

However, the good news is that the Sportotypes are broad and inclusive categories. Thus, you can apply the criteria right now to athletes you follow today to determine whether or not an athlete truly fulfills a Sportotype or not.

KEYS TO THE GAME

- *KNOW:* the euphemisms this book openly employs:

- *Race* = mostly black male players

- *Sport* = primarily top earning NFL & NBA leagues

- *Press* = overwhelmingly white-dominated press

- *Racial Rivalry* = history encapsulating institutional and systemic exclusion of blacks by whites from competing for American Dream

MENACE 2 SOCIETY

Sportotype #1

Sportotypes					
Menace 2 Society	Diva	Intellectually Suspect	Model Citizen	Comic Relief	Buck
Sportotypes Corresponding with Unholy Trinity					
FEAR			FASCINATION		
Negrophobia	Femininity	Romantic Racialism	Negrophobia	Femininity	Romantic Racialism
Sportotypes Corresponding with Rigged Game Goals					
POWER			CONTROL		
Misread Defenses to the Unholy Trinity					
Consistency	Competition	Catharsis	Consistency	Competition	Catharsis

PLAYING HARD BALL

As said earlier, sports are so beloved since they have all the trappings of an Italian Opera or Greek Drama. In both engrossing scenarios, we have heroes for which we cheer, and conversely, villains for whom we must jeer. The sports landscape is no different. Just consider how in contrast to just about every man, woman and child you meet that is genuinely enthralled with the Philadelphia Eagles, you have other teams and sports figures that the public genuinely "loves to hate." Sure, all teams are professional, yet, when you mention the New York Yankees of baseball, the Los Angeles Lakers of basketball, the New England Patriots of football, or the Edmonton Oilers of hockey, it appears that while they enjoy national fan bases outside of their geographic region, they also are polarizing teams that enjoy extra scrutiny and criticism. All in the name of good fun, perhaps.

It is no different for individual athletes. The *Menace 2 Society* Sportotype is a villainous character trope portrayed as possessing a value system that poses a threat to civil "normalcy," either through violence (or potential violence) and/or moral corruption. Threats can range from mild, socially impolite acts to dangerous, physical threats. While this text is not an exegesis on crime and its relative harm, a quick survey of news media reveals a significant number of stories concerning the "bad/criminal behavior" of professional athletes concern black NBA and NFL players. The MLB and NHL really do not have the same criminal "image" problem, at least not to the extent that the NFL and NBA do — two of the top revenue earning sports that just happen to have a majority of black players (think of criticisms lobbied by the press calling the NFL the "National Felons League").[1] Do white players in the NHL or MLB commit less crimes? Or does the white press just report on black & brown transgressions more often?

Thus, we must interrogate the resulting "chicken-and-egg" scenario whereby NBA and NFL "news" routinely includes references to mild offenses such as failing to change a driver's license address.[2] In receiving constant negative attention for transgressions, the sphere of personal autonomy for nonwhite athletes shrinks while expanding the confines of the professional "workplace." Talk radio callers flood the airwaves consistently with references to themselves having "real jobs" and it provides moral authority for them to say how they are responsible for their job — after waiting for over an hour on hold to make their commentary on the Jim Rome show during the middle of a work day, mind you.[3] Yet, due to the heightened emphasis of black athletes behaving badly, the zone of professional responsibility has now extended to "da club" at 2:00 am on weekends during offseason. With social media growing and expanding, anything a player does is essentially the "property" of the franchise and owner.

Compare this relationship that other high-earning entertainers have with their employers. A-list Hollywood Actors work on one film at a time, but are not necessarily beholden to one particular studio the way a player is beholden to a particular franchise. How hard a professional entertainer wishes to "entertain themselves" during private time has nothing to do with showing up and delivering lines when it is time for shooting. To wit, with professional sports players, one can make the argument that the number of dollar bills an athlete throws in the air to "make it rain" at a strip club has nothing to do with how well they can catch balls in the rain during game day. But now, such behavior matters.

BLACK BALLED

Bearing the long-standing racial rivalry in mind, one major source of tension has been the negotiation of power and control between white men and black men. Nowhere is this tension likely more apparent than in the realm of crime and punishment, where power and control must be exercised by the system upon the individual. While laws are theoretically created to function systematically, in practice, these laws must be individually applied to real people and scenarios. The gap between such theory and practice can vary widely given the amount of discretion and subjectivity that is part and parcel of the larger human experience. "Justice" is therefore relative.

It follows, when analyzing criminal or threatening behavior within a professional sports context, the root core of this construct is white dominated sports media being the "judge and jury" in utilizing discretion and subjectivity in deciding how to frame or report "bad behavior" by black males.[4] Mere reported black *contact* with the criminal justice system is not necessarily *bona fide* proof of actual black criminality given the dubious history of blacks and the law.

While our criminal justice system is in fact premised upon the theoretical principle of justice for all, in practice, justice for all *some of the time* has been a more accurate description. For instance, now, our society has the benefit of hindsight to see that the Era of Enslavement was an abhorrent and dark chapter of our nation's history. Fine. But during that time, police played an active role in protecting the "property" of the tax paying citizens, or slave holders, who were largely responsible for their police salaries. Enslaved persons who held bizarre thoughts of escaping their living torture and left plantations in search of American principles of "freedom" were not only diagnosed as having diseased thoughts of the mind,[5] but were literally hounded with hounds and tracked and chased down on horseback. Legally.

The police and the law were acting in cahoots to preserve a legal dynamic we now know to be problematic at the very least. White men sought to continue exercising power and control over black males after the Era of Enslavement with the advent of the Black Codes, which in the name of legal justice, severely restricted the movements of black males to help "keep them in their place" and maintain the slanted power dynamic in existence during the Era of Enslavement.[5] Black males were lawfully prosecuted for the most minor of offenses and then were consumed by the Convict Lease System whereupon they had to work off their debts to society — back on struggling plantations owned by white males who paid white male judges for referrals.[6] Lest we forget, vigilante "justice" was also meted out locally through illegal lynch mobs and domestic terrorist groups such as the Ku Klux Klan, which peaked at over four million members during the 1920s.[7]

More recent manifestations of questionable legal justice comprise the 100:1 sentencing ratio for crack versus powdered cocaine[0] when the crack cocaine epidemic exploded on the national scene during the 1980's "War on Drugs." Such a war, more aptly could be retitled a "War on Thugs," since over 90% of crack cocaine convictions with mandatory minimum federal sentences were black males in contrast to 90% of powder cocaine convictions that were white males who would only receive the same sentence if caught with 100 times the amount despite inconclusive evidence to demonstrate that crack cocaine was more dangerous.[8] Unlike the "party" or "recreational" reputation that powder cocaine enjoys inside of private residences and bathroom stalls inside swanky clubs, crack cocaine was perceived as more violent with the sensationalized media accounts of public, inner city violence associated with crack deals gone bad. The fight to uphold "law and order" and "get tough on crime" and "take back our streets" all supported the continued one-sided rivalry for power and control over black male bodies/behaviors. Such strong rhetoric pales in comparison to more recent calls for a gentler social approach now that hard drug users (e.g., heroin and meth) have white faces.[9]

We say all this to say that black male athletes consistently framed by white dominated sports media as Menaces 2 Society must be called into question and analyzed for potential bias or racial rivalry tendencies. Based upon general laws of average, blacks commit crimes just like everyone else. The question is whether blacks are prosecuted and punished like everyone else?[10] History has consistently shown that blacks found in conflict with the law were not necessarily in conflict with *justice*. That which was *legal* in this country was not always synonymous with that which was *just*.

JUST FOR SPORT

In the ten examples that follow, consider the Unholy Trinity and how they may inform or influence coverage of the story outlined. Examples of the Menace 2 Society Sportotype include, but are not limited to:

Menace to Society Example #1			
Athlete (race)	Sport/ League	Situation	When
Tiger Woods (black) NOTE: see endnote #11	PGA	In the wake of "the incident," pop culture mag "Vanity Fair" published cover photographs of Mr. Woods "in the rough."	March 2010

SOURCE: http://www.vanityfair.com/culture/2010/02/tiger-woods-201002

BRIEF ANALYSIS: Two details to observe here: 1) Mr. Woods was not depicted with golf clubs or anything golf related as he was shirtless, had a black "beanie" or wool hat without a lid and had weights in his hands — in other words, in a significant departure from the prim and pristine images typically produce of Mr. Woods up until the time of "the incident," Mr. Woods looked more like a member of the "prison weights club" as opposed to the "country club" and 2) the photos were taken six months before, or alternatively stated, *four months* before "the incident" by prize-winning photographer Anne Liebowitz but were only released *after* "the incident" speaking to how once Mr. Woods transgressed he was immediately cast within the image of the more familiar trope of the menacing black male that Mr. Woods never embraced during his career.

Menace to Society Example #2

Athlete (race)	Sport/ League	Situation	When
Ryan Moats (black)	NFL	Moats was pulled over by a police cruiser for failure to wait for a traffic light to change, the interaction was captured by dashcam.	March 2009

SOURCE: https://www.youtube.com/watch?v=_qTiu7rAS4Q

BRIEF ANALYSIS: The officer involved has since made the rare move of publicly apologizing to Moats as the video speaks for itself. Power and control are the apparent goals of the officer who at one point had his gun drawn and threatened to "mess him up" and "charge Moats with fleeing" even though they were inside of the hospital parking lot — the same hospital where Moats' mother-in-law was dying. Moats was rushing to get his wife to have one last moment with her mother once they received the urgent call from the hospital nurse. Moats' mother-in-law passed away while Moats was still being lectured by officer Robert Powell.

Menace to Society Example #3

Athlete (race)	Sport/ League	Situation	When
Ray Armstrong (black)	NFL	Player facing felony charges for allegedly threatening police dog pre-NFL game.	November 2015

SOURCE: http://espn.go.com/nfl/story/_/id/14100069/ray-ray-armstrong-oakland-raiders-investigated-allegedly-taunting-k-9

BRIEF ANALYSIS: The player was in the tunnel leading to the football field getting "hype" before the game and barked at the dog and lifted his shirt and slapped his chest. For whatever it is worth, the officer holding the dog was a white female. If you were the District Attorney, would you prosecute this act as criminal behavior? Why or why not?

Menace to Society Example #4

Athlete (race)	Sport/ League	Situation	When
Adrian Peterson (black)	NFL	Peterson received a year-long suspension for applying corporal punishment to his son.	Fall 2014

SOURCE: http://sports.yahoo.com/news/vikings-peterson-avoids-jail-plea-agreement-201652876--nfl.html

BRIEF ANALYSIS: Similar to Ray Rice, Minnesota Vikings all-pro running back Adrian Peterson committed an act that became a flash point of national discussion of corporal punishment specifically and black culture generally. Even the Governor of Minnesota weighed in on Peterson's questionable conduct — not unlike the Governor of New York who did not comment on Brett Favre and his 2011 sexual harassment case. High-ranking political officials do not always find the time to comment on matters involving high-profile professional athletes. For whatever it is worth, corporal punishment is indeed legal and Peterson did not draft nor pass the laws that make it legal in every state. Yet, Peterson did spark a national debate when he decided to employ it.[12]

Menace to Society Example #5

Athlete (race)	Sport/ League	Situation	When
Ray Rice (black)	NFL	Ray Rice struck his spouse, Janay Rice as captured by a casino elevator camera.	Summer 2014

SOURCE: http://www.sbnation.com/nfl/2014/5/23/5744964/ray-rice-arrest-assault-statement-apology-ravens

BRIEF ANALYSIS: Former Baltimore Ravens running back Ray Rice must atone and must pay for this act. Mainstream media must also be consistent in highlighting domestic violence wherever it rears its ugly head. The uncontrovertible video was a factor in galvanizing the public, yet the Rice case was a national flashpoint for awareness, debates about forgiveness, television re-enactments and Presidential statements[13] unlike prior high profile cases. *NOTE*: virtually all of the perpetrators here listed continued working after their domestic violence "scandals" blew over.

Patrick Kane		U.S. District Judge Mark Fuller	
Ben Roethlisberger		Nicolas Cage	
Hope Solo		Ozzy Osbourne	
Chuck Knoblauch		Charlie Sheen	
Bruce Miller		Sean Penn	
Bobby Cox	Sports Figures	Mickey Rourke	Non-Sports
Al Unser Jr.		Mel Gibson	Figures
Stone Cold Steve Austin		Tommy Lee	
Tom Cable		Christian Slater	
Brett Myers		James Caan	
Tony Stewart		Vanilla Ice	

In the name of consistency, did 7,000 fans line up to exchange their Ben Roethlisberger jerseys after his second attempted rape charge?[14] Ray Rice, like everyone else on the above list, must be accountable and atone. Consistency is key.

Menace to Society Example #6

Athlete (race)	Sport/ League	Situation	When
Vernon Davis (black)	NFL	Davis broke up a potential touchdown pass thrown in the general area of two receivers.	Fall 2014

SOURCE:http://sports.yahoo.com/blogs/nfl-shutdown-corner/vernon-davis-broke-up-what-would-have-been-teammate-s-first-career-td--video-041008197.html

BRIEF ANALYSIS: This is a more subtle example of a black player "doing something wrong" — even though he actually tried to do good. Sure, in a professional game where a touchdown may not be scored at all, catching a touchdown pass is an important task. Yet, whether in jest or tongue in cheek or not, this hypercriticism of black athletes by white dominated sports media is hardly ever reversed on a mainstream scale. In this article, there is no mentionable analysis of the quarterback's throw and the quality thereof. Instead, the author takes time to criticize other actions made by Davis during the game, including the fact that "he also dropped at least two passes, missed two blocks on short-yardage failures, was called for a false start and almost caused an interception by running a crummy route on the first play of the game."

Menace to Society Example #7

Athlete (race)	Sport/ League	Situation	When
Michael Vick (black)	NFL	Vick was prosecuted for financing a dog-fighting ring in Virginia.	July 2007

SOURCE: http://espn.go.com/nfl/story/_/id/13519067/protesters-speak-pittsburgh-steelers-signing-michael-vick

BRIEF ANALYSIS: In modern day parlance, Vick's name is virtually synonymous with "dogfighting." Vick served one of the longest dogfighting sentences in U.S. history, was suspended, lived in a half-way house, performed hundreds of hours in community service and was sued to repay "guaranteed money" from his contract with the Atlanta Falcons. Protests were held seven years after his prison release when signed as a backup quarterback to Ben Roethlisberger in Fall of 2015.[15] The National Organization for Women did not similarly stage a national protest against "Big Ben" Roethlisberger's first game back from his reduced suspension for sexually assaulting a second woman. Again, consistency is key.[16]

Menace to Society Example #8

Athlete (race)	Sport/ League	Situation	When
Richard Sherman (black)	NFL	Sherman emoted during interview by white female sideline reporter Erin Andrews less than two minutes after making a key defensive play to help his team make the Super Bowl.	January 2014

SOURCE:http://sports.yahoo.com/news/here-s-why-seahawks--richard-sherman-was-right-in-taking-offense-to-being-called-a-thug-233112814-nfl.html

BRIEF ANALYSIS: Sherman himself called into question the euphemism of referring to him as a "thug" in the aftermath of his stellar late-game heroics during the 2014 NFC Championship Game. A Stanford graduate, tensions arose around the perception that he made a white female reporter Erin Andrews "uncomfortable."[17] Here, power and control tensions are inflamed since the viewing audience wants to be entertained by watching Sherman play with passion, but is not equally as interested in hearing his passion personally communicated.

Menace to Society Example #9

Athlete (race)	Sport/ League	Situation	When
Thabo Sefolosha (black)	NBA	Sefolosha had his leg broken during a forceful arrest by NYC police.	April 2015

SOURCE: https://www.yahoo.com/sports/blogs/nba-ball-dont-lie/thabo-sefolosha-says his season-ending--injury-was-caused-by-the-police-193049399.html

BRIEF ANALYSIS: Sefolosha sustained a "season-ending injury" during the his team's, the Atlanta Hawks, playoff run. Sefolosha's account was validated by a court of law that found he was offering assistance to a homeless person and was roughly and unlawfully detained once he was perceived as a threat.[18] Charges of disorderly conduct and resisting arrest against Sefolosha were thrown out after a two-day trial and acquittal. His accompanying white teammate, Pero Antic was both unscathed and not arrested. Bystander cell phone video of the incident appears to show a NYPD officer swingning a baton at Sefolosha's leg after he was wrestled to the ground: https://www.youtube.com/watch?v=csR2v1SAjfA.

Menace to Society Example #10

Athlete (race)	Sport/ League	Situation	When
LeBron James (black)	NBA	James, as a free agent, chose to sign with the Miami Heat as opposed to resigning with the Cleveland Cavaliers.	July 2010

SOURCE: http://sports.yahoo.com/news/cavaliers-took-down-insane-comic-154750438.html

BRIEF ANALYSIS: Said James was blamed for the threatening of an entire economy (as if that is his responsibility and not elected city officials or the team owner), his jersey was burned and people delivered all types of insults, many of a racial nature — curious seeing how so many of these very same angry persons were "fans" of his up until "The Decision." LeBron rhetorically questioned aloud during the aftermath: "If the Cavs would have got rid of me at one point, would my family burn down the organization? Of course not. This is a business."[19]

Yet, James appeared to have committed a crime against the CORPORATE body. In the world of "free" agency, it appears only owners truly have "freedom" to make decisions about future careers and income as evidenced by the condescending tone adopted by owner Dan Gilbert in his open letter posted to the Cleveland Cavalier fans online, complete in Comic Sans font.

Ironically, in the same city, in 2013, Cleveland Browns running back Trent Richardson learned that he would be playing for a new team, not by virtue of a decision of free will, but rather: "I turned on the radio, and all of a sudden I heard, 'Cleveland Browns running back has been traded to the Colts.' It just hit me in my face like I can't believe … I didn't see it coming."[20]

Unlike St. Louis Rams fans who knew for some time that owner Sam Kroenke was planning a relocation move back to Los Angeles in 2016. Rather than one individual, an entire franchise moved and barely generated a fraction of the media coverage that Mr. James did with his "Decision" to make a change. Arguments thrown out at James over wrecking an entire regional economy actually may be applicable in this case, but with perhaps a few more jerseys to burn.

Keys to the Game

- *KEY WORDS:* urban, thug (Richard Sherman), inner city, "off the field incidents," "plays angry," "troubled player"

- On the flip side, is the third time the charm? http://sports.yahoo.com/blogs/olympics-fourth-place-medal/michael-phelps-arrested-for-dui-in-baltimore-162827931.html

4

DIVA

Sportotype #2

Sportotypes					
Menace 2 Society	Diva	Intellectually Suspect	Model Citizen	Comic Relief	Buck
Sportotypes Corresponding with Unholy Trinity					
FEAR			FASCINATION		
Negrophobia	Femininity	Romantic Racialism	Negrophobia	Femininity	Romantic Racialism
Sportotypes Corresponding with Rigged Game Goals					
POWER			CONTROL		
Misread Defenses to the Unholy Trinity					
Consistency	Competition	Catharsis	Consistency	Competition	Catharsis

PLAYING SOFT BALL

If the Menace 2 Society Sportotype represents the athlete that fans "hate to love," then the *diva* may compete for the athlete that fans "love to hate." This Sportotype is this athlete is often burlesqued, emasculated or denigrated for actions that are negatively framed as selfish and individualistic. This "attitude" is what makes him a "cancer" in the locker room to all of the other dutiful, faithful athletes who agree to behave (money and attention being the primary currencies and motivations for compliant behavior).

What makes the Diva truly problematic is that he in actuality, is not chastened by such criticisms. The diva label is applied to those athletes who not only are gifted and accomplished, but they are gifted and accomplished athletes who *know* that they are gifted and accomplished. Knowing that the window of marketability and pleasure seeking is limited, they consciously seek to maximize their window and leverage all the positive attention they can get for themselves.

What adds (...wait for it) insult to injury, is that Diva is a term of emasculation.

There is nothing inherently deficient about individuals who appear or present as effeminate in their mannerisms, dress or dealings. Sports, however, particularly the top revenue generating sports of football and basketball, are largely governed by a "macho" culture. Meaning, masculinity is stressed, valued and prized. The big money sports involve actions that often involve imposing one's will over another (e.g., blocking another for a tackle, boxing someone out for a rebound) as opposed to utilizing finesse or precision (e.g., tucking one's knees for a perfect 3.5 rotations before diving into the water). While shooting free throws and kicking long field goals involve accuracy and precision, the games of football and basketball cannot be played without physically making contact with one's opponent.

Masculinity and the display of one's masculinity is also a key part of athlete acceptance. This is part of the reason why Michael Sam's entree into the NFL was such a big story in 2014. Not that he was necessarily the first gay player in the NFL, but is credited with being the first to publicly proclaim his sexual orientation. This admission was disruptive of the prevailing narrative of heterosexual male machismo culture which is still dominant. Many speculate that he had the talent necessary to compete, but that teams passed on providing him a true opportunity to play due to this perceived "fear."[1]

Thus, within this world of male machismo, for male sports writers and journalists to refer to another heterosexual male as a "diva," this term can be very pejorative and insulting — especially for a male who publicly identifies himself and his earning potential based upon his perceived macho masculinity.

The Diva Sportotype has us consider: Are white MLB and NHL players criticized with the same frequency and fervor as black NBA and NFL players for being selfish? And if not, is it because black players are objectively more selfish? Or are actions expressed by black players perceived by white sports media as more selfish more often than not?

UNNECESSARY ROUGHNESS

But consider — if *you* were a nonwhite athlete suffering from the detrimental effects of the Unholy Trinity (e.g., constantly questioned, scrutinized, challenged, marginalized, belittled, suspected, assaulted, etc.), how would you respond when given the opportunity to express yourself on a national stage after accomplishing a major achievement?

Before answering this query, let us also recall how sports are Cathartic and immediately gratifying for many who participate within them, most especially at the professional level where one's personal livelihood is directly related to one's performance. For many of these black athletes, eluding and shedding would-be tacklers en route to a seventy-nine yard touchdown run elicits different feelings than those generated from expertly maneuvering a steering wheel during a 200-lap NASCAR race.[2] The length of time involved and amount of exertion on the body in the football example, combined with the sustained degree of difficulty builds up an investment within the body that may be released upon achievement.[3] Further, more than mere bragging rights are at stake if an athlete makes "a good play" — career trajectories, family welfare and future earning potential all can be affected by the strength of one's last play. While most reasonable fans will concur that celebration, for instance, is allowable and expected within a professional context, the pressing, subjective question becomes "how much is too much?" This is a question largely framed and answered by our white dominated sports media.

Criticisms of professional black athletes are "fair game" and should not be censored. However, our focus concerns the gray zone of hypercriticism. History instructs that black males have been constantly scrutinized and analyzed — often by educated, well-placed and respected white males — which in retrospect sounds circumspect. For example, medical doctor Dr. Samuel Cartwright "diagnosed" the disease of Drapetomia in blacks during the 1840s.[4] Drapetomia? Yes, this is the disease of enslaved individuals desirous to flee to freedom. Upon the end of enslavement in 1865, new laws were created by

Southern states entitled "Black Codes" which criminalized seemingly innocuous behaviors such as standing on a street corner without a job — which was quite common for individuals recently emancipated who found considerable difficulty finding employment from proprietors who flat out refused to hire them.[5] Also, in the post-Reconstruction era, many whites bitterly complained about the *impudence* of newly emancipated blacks who would strut about downtown in their new clothes, thinking that they were better than what they were.[6]

In other words, the impudent negro would not "stay in his place."

We must interrogate to what degree the Diva Sportotype and the criticisms associated with it hearken back to this very same concept under the principles of Racism 2.0. Meaning, to what degree are black male athletes criticized precisely because they step outside of the box of Romantic Racialism where they are most liked as tamed and behaved Model Citizens, or humble no-nonsense athletes who relentlessly sacrifice for the team and continue to work hard for the franchise and unfailingly remember to recognize the average fan. The professional sports context raises the stakes because the high salaries black male athletes receive often "liberates" them from having to comport to rules and structure — or at least some may mistakenly believe this, for in the end, "the House always wins."[7] One must eventually pay for such freedom. In other words, income + independence = impudence.

Diva is thus a term of emasculation that fulfills the average fan's desire for *schadenfreude*, or the extraction of pleasure at another's misfortune. Readers of tabloids exercise this similar pleasure when they are able to judge the "poor" high-priced fashion choices that multi-millionaires they will never meet decided to wear. Similarly, to the extent that Diva athletes are exposed and excoriated, the message is clear that no man is bigger than the game. Let alone a black man.

Yet, do consider carefully what the Diva means to both the athlete and the media. To the media, the Diva is an arrogant annoyance that must be humbled and put in their rightful place. But to the athlete, consider what an expressive statement of triumph might mean based upon our analysis of catharsis. Is the "Diva" athlete not saying: "Look at me! I matter! I did it! *I am somebody!* I am successful! I am worthy of dignity, humanity and respect!" Such activity can be viewed as a plea.

After all, no disrespect, but... any one of us can *theoretically* swing a bat, kick a soccer ball set in the ground as part of a penalty kick or set a volleyball up in the air. We did not say that we all can do these things *successfully or expertly,* but despite the low percentages, just about any able-bodied person can at least *attempt* these tasks. We *cannot* say the same about dunking a basketball on a rim ten feet high *after* rotating our bodies 360 degrees in the air or breaking four tackles en route to outrunning other elite athletes for seventy-nine yards. Physically, whether able-bodied or not, all cannot attempt or complete these tasks. Period. So for those who do, do so consistently and expertly, and not only reach this bar of physical excellence, but exceed it — well, perhaps we should consider how there *might* be some measure of self-satisfaction and gratification involved. After all, such victories *must be* contextualized in an over-arching competition for dignity and respect (think Unholy Trinity) whereby the presumption is incompetence and failure. Such failure might not be personal (think of *rigged games*), but may be taken personally nonetheless....

Just for Sport

In the ten examples that follow, consider the Unholy Trinity and how they may inform or influence coverage of the story outlined. Examples of the Diva Sportotype include, but are not limited to:

Diva Example #1

Athlete (race)	Sport/ League	Situation	When
Tiger Woods (black)	PGA	Mr. Woods' former caddie celebrated his first win over Tiger and taunted Tiger in retaliation for being too haughty during his prime.	Summer 2011

SOURCE: http://www.dailymail.co.uk/sport/golf/article-3298816/Caddie-Steve-Williams-claims-treated-like-slave-Tiger-Woods-explosive-new book.html

BRIEF ANALYSIS: Steve Williams attempted to put Tiger "back in his place" by taunting and gloating over Mr. Woods' downfall after their acrimonious split from *twelve* years of working together on the tour. He proclaimed his first win post-Tiger with Adam Scott was the best win of his career ever claiming that, "My aim was to shove it right up that black ass." He meant no offence. He was upset he was treated "like a slave."

Diva Example #2

Athlete (race)	Sport/ League	Situation	When
Terrell Owens (black)	NFL	T.O. had an ongoing public "spat" with then Philadelphia Eagles quarterback Donovan McNabb.	Fall 2004

SOURCE:http://profootballtalk.nbcsports.com/2016/02/07/why-no-t-o-in-hall-of-fame/

BRIEF ANALYSIS: T.O. did not receive the benefit of the doubt from the media and was immediately characterized afterwards as a "locker room cancer" due to his willingness to engage (or create) conflict during a game. T.O. may or may not have been the best teammate ever to walk the planet, but in his immediate defense, the question is whether the media is equally as critical of public displays of passion. Under the rubric of *power & control*, it raises the question of who has the ability to emote and be frustrated, especially when (white) Pro Bowl quarterbacks can destroy tablets during games (http://www.nfl.com/videos/nfl-game-highlights/0ap3000000576540/Aaron-Rodgers-throws-tablet-in-disgust).

Diva Example #3

Athlete (race)	Sport/ League	Situation	When
Desean Jackson (black)	NFL	Jackson is described as "attention-seeking."	Fall 2014

SOURCE: http://sports.yahoo.com/blogs/nfl-shutdown-corner/desean-jackson-on-trade-block--but-philadelphia-eagles-might-have-to-cut-him-190748678.html

BRIEF ANALYSIS: Jackson's name was in circulation for a (then-unheard of) deal to trade him out of Philadelphia, but was described in the accompanying article as "attention seeking." The phrase is not explained, nor placed in context doing more to underscore historical presumptions that a flashy black wide receiver has too large an ego that needs to be reigned into control, elsewise, he may bring unwanted "drama" to bear. Conduct an online search to see how many other white athletes have been similarly and specifically described as "attention seeking."

Diva Example #4

Athlete (race)	Sport/ League	Situation	When
Jenrry Mejía (Latino)	MLB	Known as an "animated" reliever, Mejía celebrated a bit too much after earning a save to win the game.	September 2014

SOURCE:http://sports.yahoo.com/blogs/mlb-big-league-stew/jenrry-mejia-annoys-nationals-with-postgame-celebration-201523011.html

BRIEF ANALYSIS: The Menace 2 Society threat intersects with the Diva Sportotype where such selfish "offenses" by black or Latino players can be found to have violated some of the "unwritten rules" of baseball. It is quite common to see plenty of hand wringing and pearl clutching over "disrespectful" behaviors such as flipping bats or taking too long to admire one's handiwork after hitting a home run. Toronto Blue Jays slugger Jose Bautista similarly received an onslaught of media attention in the wake of his celebratory bat flip at a crucial moment that helped propel his team further into the playoffs in October of 2015.

Diva Example #5

Athlete (race)	Sport/ League	Situation	When
LeGarette Blount (black)	NFL	Blount expressed his frustration over lack of playing time.	Fall 2015

SOURCE:http://sports.yahoo.com/blogs/nfl-shutdown-corner/legarrette-blount-suspended-for-first-game-of-2015-season-210342875.html

BRIEF ANALYSIS: "Before Blount threw a *tantrum* over a lack of playing time and got himself cut from the Steelers, he was arrested along with Bell last August for possession of marijuana" (emphasis added). Tantrum is a word typically used to describe the actions of immature children. Here the adult black male is "put in his place" via stern language from a white male writer whose own personal life is presumptively above reproach.

Diva Example #6

Athlete (race)	Sport/ League	Situation	When
Serena Williams (black)	USTA	Williams received criticism for her criticism of U.S. Open officials with whom she disagreed.	September 2009

SOURCE:http://www.theguardian.com/sport/2009/sep/13/serena-williams-tirade-us-open

BRIEF ANALYSIS: The Serena Williams outburst is immediately interpreted as combative, not competitive in contrast to white male tennis player John McEnroe's famous and lengthy tirades; an anger that is now "marketable" as the substance of whimsical commercials (https://www.youtube.com/watch?v=uVYP99dIAyo). Williams may in fact could have used better language in addressing the line judge. Can the media use better language in addressing Serena? The ultimate irony is that McEnroe has gone on record criticizing Serena for not showing "*people in the sport* a little more respect." See http://abcnews.go.com/Sports/story?id=100522&page=1. Hmm. Let's briefly analyze. There are primarily white people in the class conscious sport of tennis. Impudence strikes again; game, set, match.

Diva Example #7

Athlete (race)	Sport/ League	Situation	When
Usain Bolt (black)	Olympics	Bolt broke world record for 100m dash in grand style, was criticized by IOC President Jacques Rogge for not showing "more respect."	Summer 2008

SOURCE: http://www.huffingtonpost.com/2008/08/21/ioc-slams-usain-bolt-for_n_120397.html

BRIEF ANALYSIS: Black Jamaican sprinter Usain Bolt not only broke the world record in the 100 meter dash, but he did so while tapping his chest and looking behind at the competition he left behind. Some were slack jawed over Bolt's bravado and style while others were tight lipped. International Olympic Committee President Jacques Rogge did not appreciate Bolt's "showboating" and commented publicly accordingly. However, it is unknown whether he has also gone on record for the white dominated sport of snowboarding where hot dogging cost white American Lindsey Jacobellis the Olympic gold medal. See: http://espn. go.com/figure-skating/winter06/snowboard/columns/story?id=2334018.

Diva Example #8

Athlete (race)	Sport/ League	Situation	When
Robert "Bob" Johnson (black)	NBA	Johnson was criticized for being narcissistic in supposedly naming franchise after himself.	Fall 2004

SOURCE: http://www.atthehive.com/2014/5/3/5677830/charlotte-bobcats-original-branding-bob-johnson-hornets

BRIEF ANALYSIS: Johnson was criticized consistently for naming a new NBA franchise the Charlotte Bobcats (Michael Jordan changed the name back to Hornets in 2014). Investigate to discover what was at issue here. After all, having the public patronize businesses named after people is not a new concept (https://en.wikipedia.org/wiki/List_of_companies_named_after_people). If anything, as the first black individual to *ever* purchase a NBA franchise, perhaps businesses named after *black people* is a new concept.

Diva Example #9

Athlete (race)	Sport/ League	Situation	When
Chad Johnson (black)	NFL	Judge gave Johnson thirty days in jail for being arrogant and disrespectful.	June 2013

SOURCE: https://www.youtube.com/watch?v=5MZ8Dy8uOho

BRIEF ANALYSIS: Chad Johnson made a court appearance for violating probation for a domestic violence case. This is sad and unfortunate. More sad and unfortunate is that upon resolving the case to avoid jail time, Johnson slapped his lawyer on the butt, akin to how players indicate "good play" when out on the field of play (how this tradition started is the subject of another chapter). The white female judge was none too amused and therefore sentenced Johnson to thirty days in jail. Johnson was promptly handcuffed and led away. While the pretext for Johnson's presence in the courtroom are disturbing, so is the context for Johnson's removal from the courtroom See: https://www.youtube.com/watch?v=5MZ8Dy8uOho. The judge in an unquestioned display of power in response to public embarrassment, obtained instant "justice" by teaching the impudent negro to "stay in his place." Or jail.

Diva Example #10

Athlete (race)	Sport/ League	Situation	When
Allen Iverson (black)	NBA	A.I. responded to criticism that he was not being mature enough to treat practice seriously.	Fall 2002

SOURCE: https://www.youtube.com/watch?v=eGDBR2L5kzI

BRIEF ANALYSIS: Famously referred to as the "practice rant," NBA All-Star and bottle-of-lightning phenom Allen Iverson finally could not take it anymore. After being dogged by the media for missing practice, the implication that he was not taking his job seriously and was being selfish in thinking only about his welfare at the expense of his work ethic, Iverson struck back. Iverson attempted to point out the logical lapse in the media focusing upon missed practices rather than games made (and won!). "We sittin' up here talkin' 'bout practice!" is now the stuff of legend.

KEYS TO THE GAME

- *KEY WORDS:* immature, maturity, "needs to be managed," ego, "needs to tone it down," "plays with emotion," "me-first attitude," "prima donna," enablers, showboating, "celebrating too much," "locker room cancer," selfish, discipline

- In light of our earlier exposition of the concept of Catharsis and the "unwritten rules of baseball," re-evaluate these three areas where players are officially regulated, in part reaction from actions made by mostly black players in times past, and what do they mean within the larger context of *power & control.* Namely, think about to whom the following three policies are primarily applied in contrast to the self-regulating, unwritten policies of pitchers "brushing back" or beaning batters in MLB games to "send a message" along with the flat out acceptance of fighting as merely "part of the game" in the NHL:

  - the NFL's 15-yard Unsportmanlike Conduct penalty for an unbecoming celebration
  - the NCAA's similar 15-yard Unsportsmanlike Conduct penalty for an unbecoming celebration
  - the NBA's technical foul policy for "overt" player reactions to referee calls during the field of play

5

INTELLECTUAL

SUSPECT

Sportotype #3

Sportotypes					
Menace 2 Society	Diva	Intellectually Suspect	Model Citizen	Comic Relief	Buck
Sportotypes Corresponding with Unholy Trinity					
FEAR			FASCINATION		
Negrophobia	Femininity	Romantic Racialism	Negrophobia	Femininity	Romantic Racialism
Sportotypes Corresponding with Rigged Game Goals					
POWER			CONTROL		
Misread Defenses to the Unholy Trinity					
Consistency	Competition	Catharsis	Consistency	Competition	Catharsis

PLAYING SMART BALL

Legendary NBA player and World Champion Philadelphia 76er Julius Erving wrote the following in "Dr. J: The Autobiography":[1]

> I worry that I am not up to the task of explaining the essence of basketball as it is played at the highest levels....Because it is not a moment, it is a sense, an instinct, a flicker of insight and nerve so sudden that you have to act on it before it is a thought. What do you see? A subtle shift of weight, a lowering of the hands, a leaning forward, a glance, and that is enough to set off a chain of events. They are actions that stem from a thousand tiny instincts. But from where we are sitting above the court, we are unable to explain the game through these small moments, and instead talk about the Bulls' second chance scoring and the Rockets' bench production. I understand the need to do that, I have done some of that in this book, but I also know that we are simply describing a simulation of the game, rendering a three-dimensional activity in two dimensions.

In reading the passage above, the reader fully understands why and how this block quote was approved for insertion with this text. Julius Erving provides a cogent and insightful analysis of a series of related concepts, many of which he labors to explicate since they are so nuanced and particular requiring considerable time to parse out fully. Mr. Erving's analysis is certainly befitting of his nickname: Dr. J.

The term "dumb jock" is a bit of a misnomer for, in order to play professional sports competitively, in addition to physical talent, intellect must be present. Let us consider a running back who is to "run through the hole" that the offensive line creates for a routine running play. From the instant that the running back moves forward to receive the hand off from the quarterback, many calculations must be made — and made quickly! From judging how long the originally designated hole will stay open, to where to move next after moving into the next level of defense typically populated by bruising linebackers. All the while calculating and analyzing angles of attack, distance and rates of speed and distance by would-be oncoming tacklers. Being able to react to ever-changing scenarios requires thought at a high level, no matter how much practice one has had.

Yet, for some odd reason, the prevailing narrative is that black athletes in particular, harbor a "pure athletic skill"[2] and merely instinctively react to keep producing phenomenal plays. Such narratives differ from the praise routinely heaped upon white athletes who present as "students of the game" (e.g., baseball players who deduce the "right pitch" to obtain a ground out). *Intellectual Suspect* Sportotypes are sports figures that occupy positions of authority or esteem (e.g., quarterback, coach, etc.), but find their "expertise" undermined, thereby rendering their authority as mostly symbolic in nature. These larger than life figures are primarily cut down to size for: 1) Poor Plays, 2) Failed Finances and 3) Poor Political Plays.

Poor Plays

It is inevitable that even the greatest amongst the greats will prove mortal and make mistakes over time. The issue here is not that any nonwhite athlete is above critique or reproach; but often, the athlete's "mistake" is merely a foil to open the door to deep-seated narratives that hearken back to the Unholy Trinity. Hardly are athletes within white-dominated sports such as swimming, skiing and golf criticized for "not being motivated" or displaying "poor work ethic" the way black players in football and basketball have.[3] Such critiques have been levied against blacks since the beginning of their "work history" as enslaved within America.[4]

In developing the theme of "impudence" introduced in the previous chapter's discussion about Diva Sportotypes, it is difficult to cleanly discern when common criticisms about "accountability," "being disciplined," or praises of a "well-coached team" are not masquerading as racially-coded euphemisms centered around a locus of *power & control* not as readily associated with common parlance seen in baseball or hockey. White dominated sports like tennis and golf operate on a time-honored, self-governed honor code of competition whereas the "unruly nonwhites" need to be tamed in other sports.

More data is required on this topic. Yet, when the Unholy Trinity and its historical significance to the common narrative of black male utility and value are brought to the forefront in concert with a virtual absence of commonly disseminated dignified images of black males outside of a sports/entertainment context, we must at least question whether publicly vented fantasy league criticisms of black players (for example) only stoke flames of thinly veiled racial critiques simmering underneath the surface the whole time.

Routine criticism must be juxtaposed against white intelligence as seen through the coaching and front office ranks. Routinely, white males are lauded and congratulated for excellent "play calling," for spacing the players who actually perform the plays and for being "brilliant in-game strategists."[5] Despite having had mediocre professional playing careers (if any), many white males are consistently able to demonstrate their intellectual grasp of the game. Additionally, the coaching ranks, front office and media have all been overwhelmingly white ever since these sports institutions first began. Suffice to be said, all of the four major sports leagues (e.g., NFL, MLB, NBA & NHL)started off as *all white* or segregated affairs. The question remains whether much has *fundamentally* changed this power dynamic despite the growth in "diversity" over the years.

Failed Finances

Here, the data is both damning and alarming. 78% of former NFL players are broke or under financial duress only two years after retiring whereas the percentage in the NBA is 60% only five years out of the league.[6] On the surface, such riches to rags stories appear inexcusable. Why or how any half-witted person would blow through millions of dollars in a matter of mere months is beyond the reasonable person's ken. Or is it? In the player's "defense," it is appropriate to ask: "Which one is it?" Do we want expert ball handlers or bond handlers? So many athletes dedicate their lives to being the best player possible, with little time to becoming the best money manager. While not a perfect excuse, it is a factor that many black athletes come from backgrounds more vulnerable to exploitation unlike other white dominated sports such as tennis, golf, hockey or skiing where a higher economic familial standing is common in order to facilitate consistent access to expensive equipment and training facilities not easily found within public parks. Families with higher economic standing may be better positioned to expose and educate the developing athlete about the "game" of finances in addition to the "game" of sports.

Not to mention, a hard-charging competitive drive on the field that spurned an individual to defy odds and become a professional basketball player may also carry over off the field vis a vis spending habits and risky investments. Plus, in light of the old adage, "It takes 20 years to make an overnight success," by the time an individual makes it to the professional ranks of basketball or football, it is true that these individuals actually have been *working* at their craft for close to two decades! After finally achieving success, other observers — many who have not even "played the game" at a competitive level, now become self-deputized experts on how another should manage not just their money, but even more complex, one's life-long dreams.

Poor Political Plays

Occasionally, the two worlds of sport and reality will intersect and collide. It is not uncommon that when these two worlds do so through the bodies of black males, that revulsion results. When black players remind us that they are human and have political views outside of their job scope — particularly when related to political issues centered around black males — players are promptly reminded of "their place" and are discouraged from "confusing the public" with the brand they represent on the front of their jersey versus the brand of politics they represent on the back.[7]

Despite the fact that the dark cloud of the Unholy Trinity may be the "white elephant" in the room, serving as a subtext and context for how black players exist, these professional players still have a "job to do."

NICKELING & DIMING THE QUARTERBACK

Nowhere do we see this dynamic quite so explicit and direct but in the black quarterback. Similar to Tuskegee Airmen who were flat out rejected due to the conclusion they were "mental inferior subspecies of the human race"[8] and therefore incapable of handling expensive military machinery, similar observations are made by those who cast aspersions on black quarterbacks.[9]

Let's face it, as the literal "face" of a franchise, the marketing opportunities are different for black quarterbacks. From Doug Williams, to Warren Moon to Randall Cunningham to Steve McNair to Dante Culpepper to Michael Vick and Donovan McNabb and Cam Newton, all have been subjected to additional scrutiny along the lines of intelligence.[10]

JUST FOR SPORT

In the ten examples that follow, consider the Unholy Trinity and how they may inform or influence coverage of the story outlined. Examples of the Intellectual Suspect Sportotype include, but are not limited to:

Intellectual Suspect Example #1

Athlete (race)	Sport/ League	Situation	When
Tiger Woods (black)	PGA	Tiger had a rules violation called in to the PGA by a viewer at home.	April 2013

SOURCE: http://www.golf.com/tour-and-news/tiger-woods-drop-masters-2013-inside-story

BRIEF ANALYSIS: Rules are the rules! And Tiger was made to answer with a two-stroke penalty for an improper ball drop for an errant shot. Many believe that favoritism for (what was then) one of the most marketable players of the game shielded Tiger from full disqualification. Tiger was not shielded however, from a nationwide discussion about his knowledge of the rules. But yet, with most things Tiger, more eyes are always watching. Do fans also watch for and respect the "Tiger Woods effect?"[11]

Intellectual Suspect Example #2

Athlete (race)	Sport/ League	Situation	When
Albert Pujols (Latino)	MLB	Pujols was chided for chiding the media.	August 2014

SOURCE: http://hardballtalk.nbcsports.com/2014/08/28/albert-pujols-plays-the-you-never-played-the-game-card/?ocid=Yahoo&partner=ya5nbcs

BONUS: http://profootballtalk.nbcsports.com/2014/09/13/roddy-white-dubs-pft-complete-asswholes-for-highlighting-his-adrian-peterson-tweet/

BRIEF ANALYSIS: Arguably worse than touching the taboo analogy of "Slavery & Sport," is to attempt to criticize the critical sports media. Under the rubric of *power & control,* whenever an elite, nonwhite athlete issues a physical challenge that a "regular" white male reporter would otherwise lose, the white male "evens the playing field" and even asserts the upper hand through the "power of pen." Just like the "House always wins," the media always get the last word.

Snarky white writers get upset over players criticizing the fact that they have not played the game, or at least not at an elite professional level consistently. By asserting that one's critiques should be discounted due to a lack of *a priori* experience, Pujols reflects irritation shared by other nonwhite athletes that mere observers and non-practitioners of "the game" within media can claim moral and intellectual superiority and directly influence and affect the actual player's career as a result of such observations. It is difficult to think of another analogous scenario. Imagine: blacks and Latinos packed in the galley of a courtroom providing public critiques about the lawyering taking place by the District Attorney (DA) in front of the courtroom, making points based upon what they have seen from television legal dramas, despite having never attended law school. It is difficult to even finish this hypothetical as it is so farcical to imagine these public critiques even having an iota of influence of the next job the DA could even take.

BONUS ANALYSIS: The tension between black male athletes and white male non-athletes (who are then professional media journalists) remains vastly understudied. Famous cases of black males exhibiting "resistance" attempting to "outsmart" the media come in the form of not answering questions or in steadily repeating canned answers (see NBA's Rasheed Wallace's "both teams played hard," or NFL's Arian Foster's "be a better teammate" quotes). In response, consider, could the following words of sports media journalist Mike Florio be interpreted as a valid critique? Or could these words also be viewed as a veiled threat to correct the impudence of the ungrateful black who will not stay in his place?

> "So, yes, someone finally got through to Kaepernick that it's not in his best interests to be gratuitously combative with the media. Especially since, at some point, the media will be expressing opinions on whether the 49ers should decide, on or before April 1, whether to continue to keep Kaepernick around."[12]

Intellectual Suspect Example #3

Athlete (race)	Sport/ League	Situation	When
Lance Briggs (black)	NFL	Briggs' decision to leave practice for the opening of his restaurant was called into question.	September 2014

SOURCE: http://sports.yahoo.com/blogs/nfl-shutdown-corner/bears--lance-briggs-skipped-monday-practice-for-his-restaurant-opening-135304495.html

BRIEF ANALYSIS: Here the media questioned Briggs decision and loyalty. Briggs' partner scheduled the opening of his barbecue restaurant on Labor Day, figuring most people do not work that day. Briggs had practice ("Not a game!" "Not a game!" as Allen Iverson would say) and did what most American employees do — despite having a job to perform they make individual decisions about when they have to leave for personal matters. Just like when NFL head coaches miss practices just to escort their daughters to college.[13] Or when college football coaches reschedule official collegiate competitions for their daughter's wedding.[14]

Intellectual Suspect Example #4

Athlete (race)	Sport/ League	Situation	When
Chris Johnson (black)	NFL	Johnson's work ethic called into question.	April 2014

SOURCE: http://profootballtalk.nbcsports.com/2014/04/06/report-chris-johnsons-work-ethic-irked-titans-officials/?cid=Yahoo

BRIEF ANALYSIS: This story raises the question of whether sports media is nearly as interested in "how hard" mostly white baseball players, complete with their more liberal physiques, go all out in sprints during baseball "practice" (see Chapter 2, Diva, ex. # 10) while shagging balls and taking batting swings and occasional bunting drills. Soccer players, hockey players, volleyball players, tennis players are more shielded from the media and public scrutiny when it comes to their practices, where we trust that they are smart enough to do the right thing.

Intellectual Suspect Example #5

Athlete (race)	Sport/ League	Situation	When
Venus Williams (black)	NBA	Williams decision to take leave for illness called into question.	July 2014

SOURCE: http://www.eonline.com/news/556981/martina-navratilova-thinks-it-s-clear-that-a-virus-didn-t-cause-serena-williams-shaky-wimbledon-exit

BRIEF ANALYSIS: Serena Williams' decision to withdraw from doubles competition with her sister, Venus, was called into question by other female tennis great, Martina Navratilova. Although Serena received medical attention before they took the court and could not get her serve over the net, Navratilova stated: "I find it distressing." What is fascinating about this article is that it truly is about Navratilova's opinion and not about what Williams herself might have thought. If we are not to trust the athlete and their own relationship with their own body, then what?

Intellectual Suspect Example #6

Athlete (race)	Sport/ League	Situation	When
Chad Ochocinco (black)	NBA	Ochocinco criticized for criticizing Tom Brady.	September 2011

SOURCES: >http://articles.sun-sentinel.com/2011-09-14/sports/sfl-tedy-bruschi-rips-chad-ochocinco-11_1_chad-ochocinco-tweet-tom-brady

>http://espn.go.com/boston/nfl/story/_/id/6968925/chad-ochocinco-tweet-draws-ire-ex-new-england-patriots-player-tedy-bruschi

>http://www.youtube.com/watch?v=8Tc7h8k7Cn4 (1:05 mark)

BRIEF ANALYSIS: Essentially, in the eyes of a former white NFL player, Teddy Bruschi, Chad Johnson had not "earned the right" or was not smart enough to appreciate the hard work ethic required of success. Bruschi criticized Johnson's compliment of Brady: "Just waking up after a late arrival, I've never seen a machine operate like that n person, to see video game numbers put up in person was WOW." Said Bruschi: "Drop the awe factor.... It's amazing to see because you don't understand it! You still don't understand it and it's amazing to you because you can't get it."

Intellectual Suspect Example #7

Athlete (race)	Sport/ League	Situation	When
DeSean Jackson (black)	NBA	Jackson's decision to celebrate touchdown in losing effort questioned.	September 2014

SOURCE: http://sports.yahoo.com/news/desean-jackson-doesnt-realize-washington-224100460.html

BRIEF ANALYSIS: The headline, "DeSean Jackson doesn't realize the Washington Redsk*ns lost to the Eagles" explains the media's opinion of Jackson's intellect.

Intellectual Suspect Example #8

Athlete (race)	Sport/ League	Situation	When
Michael Jordan (black)	NBA	Jordan was criticized for poor player personnel decisions.	November 2014

SOURCE: https://www.yahoo.com/finance/news/michael-jordans-big-offseason-free-151900514.html

BRIEF ANALYSIS: This speaks to the Romantic Racialism prong of the Unholy Trinity, where Jordan, the high-flying, exhilarating dunking and scoring machine was the object of admiration and adulation whereas Jordan, the strategic executive is the object of scrutiny and scorn.

Intellectual Suspect Example #9

Athlete (race)	Sport/ League	Situation	When
Carmelo Anthony (black)	NBA	Syracuse University head basketball coach Jimmy Boheim reveals Anthony's (poor) grades.	October 2014

SOURCE: http://yahoo.thepostgame.com/blog/dish/201410/jim-boeheim-reveals-carmelo-anthonys-first-grades-college-4-cs-1-d

BRIEF ANALYSIS: Jim Boheim literally revealed Carmelo Anthony's first semester report card at Syracuse. Is this not a FERPA violation?

Intellectual Suspect Example #10			
Athlete (race)	Sport/ League	Situation	When
Vince Young (black)	NBA	Young scored poorly on the Wonderlic test during the NFL combine.	Fall 2006

SOURCE: http://espn.go.com/espn/page2/story?page=jones/060301

BRIEF ANALYSIS: Black quarterbacks have always been scrutinized and criticized for their intelligence, Mr. Young being no exception. Say what you want, but your average "village idiot" would likely face difficulty stepping in and serving as the starting quarterback of a winning College Football National Championship team.

KEYS TO THE GAME

- *KEY WORDS:* "understanding the game," "grasp the offense," "learning the system"

- Observe the rhetoric employed against NFL's Donovan McNabb by his Offensive Coordinator at the time: http://www.washingtonpost.com/wp-dyn/content/article/2010/12/23/AR2010122305826.html

- Public criticisms of black quarterbacks occur in NCAA football as well: http://sports.yahoo.com/blogs/ncaaf-dr-saturday/notre-dame-coach-brian-kelly-is-frustrated-with-qb-everett-golson-s-mistakes-215018463.html (see line about "conceptual awareness")

- This Sportotype further shrinks the sphere of personal autonomy for the black player, calling into question their true measure of *power & control;* consider how "three Cowboys staffers said there is 'concern' regarding Bryant's living arrangement, in which as many as 10 people might be living at his house" — with such concern potentially affecting contract negotiations at the time: http://www.sbnation.com/nfl/2014/11/9/7181227/dez-bryant-dallas-cowboys-contract-off-field

MODEL CITIZEN

Sportotype #4

Sportotypes					
Menace 2 Society	Diva	Intellectually Suspect	Model Citizen	Comic Relief	Buck
Sportotypes Corresponding with Unholy Trinity					
FEAR			FASCINATION		
Negrophobia	Femininity	Romantic Racialism	Negrophobia	Femininity	Romantic Racialism
Sportotypes Corresponding with Rigged Game Goals					
POWER			CONTROL		
Misread Defenses to the Unholy Trinity					
Consistency	Competition	Catharsis	Consistency	Competition	Catharsis

PLAYING GOOD BALL

The *Model Citizen* Sportotype is especially fascinating if only for the fact that this athlete technically does not exist. But much like a griffin, or mythical half-eagle, half-lion type beast, the griffin in fact does have a place within mythical lore although few in fact have been able to show persuasive proof of its existence. The Model Citizen sports figure is regarded for their social skill or ability to "play along," typically at the sacrifice of individualist critical thinking or "rebellious" tendencies. Thus, this Sportotype is more so an ideal trope or mainstream image pattern — a standard of behavior against which athletes are judged, but are hardly likely to ever reach. Set up as the contrasting ideal of the Menace 2 Society, this athlete is in a precarious position since any failure to live up to Model Citizen status will result in castigation and condemnation as a Menace 2 Society Sportotype.

With the Model Citizen, behavioral perfection is routinely expected although seldom obtained. Yet, "model" behavior by the nonwhite athlete is literally rewarded with national endorsements so that direct monetary value is assigned to marketable imagery. With the Unholy Trinity in mind, it is not uncommon to see the mainstream marketing machinery indicate its preference for "anti-stereotype" black males in the NBA and NFL who are compliant, appear non-threatening and apolitical with no criminal baggage, most especially when they literally serve as models for nationally advertised and distributed products. The larger the financial stakes, the larger the push to find a Model Citizen with whom everybody can get along.[1]

Romantic Racialism, Feminity and Negrophobia all strike again.

The value of this Sportotype is that it provides an important cathartic mental space for many white patrons, who would rather "focus on the game" and not focus upon the bitter realities facing many impoverished, desperate and undereducated black and brown youths. What may take away from the entertainment value is the painful truth that these "entertainers" are secretly desperate, and are motivated to spectacular play *in part* because sports is the only logical route to the American Dream in fulfillment of the Horatio Alger narrative.[2] While many observers of sport are at least casually aware of such a nexus, they nonetheless use the Model Citizen to project their preferences for the athlete who is able to perform/entertain with a "good attitude"[3] (e.g., "service with a smile") and their ability to manage their affairs both on and off the playing surface.

The Model Citizen Sportotype calls into question the hypercriticism that many nonwhite athletes endure. In a perverse indirect recognition of the Unholy Trinity, many understand that many black NFL & NBA athletes come from "humble origins" due in part to historicized, racialized and institutionalized structures. For instance, consider the 2013 film entitled "NFL Films Presents: The Trash-Talking Cornerback" and the accompanying description: "Seattle Seahawks cornerback Richard Sherman is known for getting in the faces of opponents and speaking his mind. Find out how his tough upbringing has inspired him to be a great person and athlete."[4] When the NFL itself uses phraseology such as "tough upbringing" to advertise its media products that showcase its human products, it is difficult to imagine a golf or water polo star being similarly promoted. Accentuating "tough" recognizes that the Unholy Trinity touched upon the life of this black male as a youth, but no further analysis or contextualization is offered as to why. Moreover, implied is that Mr. Sherman has deduced a way to channel all of his pent-up aggression from his youth into a frightfully entertaining outlet on Sunday afternoons (and not elsewhere) like a good model citizen should.

The Model Citizen is therefore appealing since part of his good deed is to shoulder the burden of "the struggle" of the Unholy Trinity with a smile — more rather, should the burden away from white patrons. The Model Citizen makes the average white consumer feel more comfortable since he is not hell bent upon reminding patrons of larger structural and political ills, especially when people are looking for a few moments of diversion. Furthermore, as paying customers, many a fan pays quite a pretty penny for high quality diversion.

Then, the implicit agreement is that in exchange for leap frogging all of the hard working "middle class" patrons that faithfully support the franchise, the athlete must "bear the cost" for such success. In other words, since many of these nonwhite athletes are indeed *professional* and are handsomely compensated, such high priced laborers should not "lower themselves" and respond to unkind exchanges with disgruntled fans — even when such "critiques" take upon a racist character. Here, the takeaway is that "the customer is always right" and earned the right to spew forth such vitriol when not aggressively policed or punished inside arenas. Many a nonwhite professional athlete has complained about enduring such indignities (especially through vicious and vulgar attacks on social media), but so far, it has just been absorbed as "part of the game." Yet, to call attention to underlying racial subtexts or even to remotely suggest that racial subtexts can possibly exist is to exhibit "poor form."

Hence, this athlete is diametrically opposed to the Menace 2 Society Sportotype. This is the athlete we can trust for he just wants to do well, buy a new home for his mama[5] and play ball "just like coach say."[6] The Model Citizen narrative allows for effective muting of the Diva Sportotype (think the University of Miami football team from the 1980s). Such dialogue and imagining is rampant at the collegiate level where older white male commentators such as, Dick Vitale, Bobby

Knight and Jay Bilas rave over players who "play the right way" and choose fundamentals over flashy, unnecessary individualistic actions (even though, those are the very acts the crowd cheers!).

Even great or superhuman athletes occasionally remind us of their humanistic and mortal tendencies. Humans often make mistakes. But responsible humans do not shirk their responsibility to the profession or occupation. At least, not in the professional sports world where the failure to publicly exhibit a desire to work hard is immediately identified and criticized. Just take a quick mental inventory about how many media stories are circulated within NHL and MLB circles about players that "do not like to practice" in contrast to NFL and NBA athletes. Sportstalk radio listeners commonly call in and rail about how "If I don't do my job…" how real world consequences are sure to follow. After waiting on hold for forty-five minutes to call in to the Jim Rome show. During the middle of a work day.[7]

For when it comes to "professional work," or compensating an individual for labor provided, it is fascinating to see and hear commoners and analysts alike scrutinizing whether nonwhite athletes are doing everything necessary to prove themselves worthy of their publicly disclosed pay scales. Seeing how such professional wages are quite high, whether fueled by jealousy or true fiscal concern, a cardinal sin that riles fans and media alike is the audacity of a nonwhite athlete "taking plays off." The Model Citizen is earnest and resolves to hustle every time since lapses in effort or concentration are all caught on film for instant analysis. Conversely, in a related, high-priced industry such as Hollywood, "mistakes" often are redone or edited out in the final production. The impromptu nature of sport does not allow for such luxury. The sphere of autonomy continues to shrink for nonwhite players in contrast to whites' general plasticity with criminality and increased sphere of autonomy outside of their entertainment profession.

JUST FOR SPORT

In the ten examples that follow, consider the Unholy Trinity and how they may inform or influence coverage of the story outlined. Examples of the Model Citizen Sportotype include, but are not limited to:

Model Citizen Example #1			
Athlete (race)	Sport/ League	Situation	When
Tiger Woods (black)	PGA	Mr. Woods apologized to the parents of his daughters pre-school classmates.	February 2010

SOURCE: http://content.usatoday.com/communities/entertainment/post/2010/02/tiger-woods-apologizes-again---to-preschool/1#.VvfHISlzeM4

BONUS SOURCE: http://sports.yahoo.com/blogs/nba-ball-dont-lie/lebron-james-sends-cupcakes-and-a-sweet-note-of-apology-to-his-neighbors-after-a-media-deluge-163551513.html

BRIEF ANALYSIS: Under the rubric of *power & control*, who was this apology truly for? Was it merely a classy gesture to recognize the increased media attention and unwanted paparazzi? Or was this move an effort to placate mostly white elite white parents who wanted to feel better about Mr. Woods being "put back in his place?" If the last hypothetical question strikes as a bit "over-the-top," what about the media's fascination with Tiger's "disappointment" to the youth of the nation and the necessity to take responsibility? At the time the scandal broke out, Tiger was directly asked in interviews whether he would be accountable enough to tell his kids — a question rarely asked of our long list of politicians and publicly elected officials who never fail to "disappoint" with their run-of-the-mill infidelity scandals.[8]

BONUS ANALYSIS: Similarly, LeBron James attempted to ingratiate himself with his neighbors by sending a note and cupcakes in response to increased media in the neighborhood to cover the story when "the prodigal son" LeBron James returned to Cleveland after a stint in Miami. Presuming James can afford to live in a well-off area, and he is an international basketball star, what does it say about the "regular" neighbors who inhabit the other expensive homes? While these "regular" names are likely better off than the average American, James can only join the new neighborhood, if he remains humble and knows his place in relation to these well-off neighbors. Even if James is better off.

Model Citizen Example #2

Athlete (race)	Sport/ League	Situation	When
Trey Burke (black)	NBA	Burke apologized for naked photos of him that were released without his authorization.	September 2014

SOURCE: http://sports.yahoo.com/blogs/nba-ball-dont-lie/why-should-trey-burke-have-to-apologize-for-taking-nude-pictures-of-himself-190505968.html

BRIEF ANALYSIS: Burke technically is the victim here. First he took photos of himself, which under "freedom of press," is his own Constitutional right to do. Next, he shared them with one individual who without his consent, decided to share them with the world. Rather than treat him like the victim he his, Burke must apologize to his owner (no pun intended) for the shame and embarrassment the situation wrought on, despite the fact that he personally was not responsible. This is further evidence of the employer sphere growing larger, while the individual sphere grows smaller.

Model Citizen Example #3

Athlete (race)	Sport/ League	Situation	When
DeMarcus Cousins (black)	NBA	Cousins praised for his maturity and contribution.	September 2014

SOURCE: http://sports.yahoo.com/blogs/nba-ball-dont-lie/jerry-colangelo-rightfully-praises-demarcus-cousins-for-his-contributions-to-team-usa-013538662.html

BRIEF ANALYSIS: Ah yes! The maturity. On your own, conduct a search to see how often the word "maturity" is used with MLB or NHL players. Even the title of the article suggests condescension or moral superiority when the white male author approves of such recognition (e.g., "rightfully praises").

Model Citizen Example #4

Athlete (race)	Sport/ League	Situation	When
Ndomakah Suh (black)	NFL	NFL's Detroit Lions hired a new head coach who then held voluntary workouts; Suh did not show while in new contract negotiations.	April 2014

SOURCE: http://sports.yahoo.com/news/ndamukong-suh-already-testing-leadership-of-lions--new-coach-with-no-show-at-voluntary-workouts-052338992.html

http://sports.yahoo.com/news/voluntary-except-180050158--nfl.html

BRIEF ANALYSIS: Why call the workouts "voluntary" if there is a consequence for not showing? While recommended, they are not required. Nothing to see here. Except for a national story about Suh "misbehaving" again.

Model Citizen Example #5

Athlete (race)	Sport/ League	Situation	When
	NBA	The NBA under David Stern's helm instituted several policies to make the product look better.	February 2014

SOURCE: http://www.sbnation.com/nba/2014/1/23/5331808/david-stern-retirement-career-retrospective-nba-commissioner

BRIEF ANALYSIS: When NBA Commissioner David Stern retired, he left behind several policies that were debated as good for the NBA image but perhaps restrictive of player personnel. Whether it was the new dress code, banning of "overt" reactions to referees or unilaterally instituting new balls without consulting the players union, Stern's decisions most always involved the tensions of *power & control* between white owners and mostly black players.

These tensions were magnified during the 2011 NBA Lockout when Miami Heat star Dwayne Wade shouted at Stern in response to what he perceived as condescension: "Don't point your finger at me...I'm not a child."[9]

Model Citizen Example #6

Athlete (race)	Sport/ League	Situation	When
Russell Westbrook (black)	NBA	Westbrook critiqued for not giving friendlier interviews.	January 2015

SOURCE: http://probasketballtalk.nbcsports.com/2015/01/17/russell-westbrook-conducts-another-hostile-postgame-interview-video/?ocid=Yahoo&partner=ya5nbcs

BRIEF ANALYSIS: Westbrook joins a long list of names that the media has deemed unfriendly over the years. Yet, the Barry Bonds or Marshawn Lynchs of the world appear to undergo a different type of scrutiny in contrast to the respectful if not humorous resignation adopted by media who find white males of influence to be difficult interviews. Compare the verbiage describing Griffin's responses: (http://sports.yahoo.com/blogs/nfl-shutdown-corner/perturbed-robert-griffin-iii-gives-same-answer-to-most-questions-174656325.html) to that of NBA's Gregg Popovich's zingers or Bill Belichick's infamous "We're on to Cincinnati" quote: (http://boston.cbslocal.com/2015/09/02/bill-belichick-on-to-cincinnati-do-your-job-video/).

Model Citizen Example #7

Athlete (race)	Sport/ League	Situation	When
LeSean McCoy (black)	NFL	McCoy criticized for not being a good citizen in shorting a restaurant tip.	September 2014

SOURCE: https://www.yahoo.com/news/lesean-mccoy-20-cent-tip-receipt-ebay-192130076.html

BONUS SOURCE: >http://sports.yahoo.com/blogs/nfl-shutdown-corner/warren-sapp-stiffs-waitress-on-a-tip--then-explains-himself-on-twitter-153631714.html

>http://www.tmz.com/2014/09/15/floyd-mayweather-tip-waitress-stiffed-las-vegas-fight-marcos-maidana/

BRIEF ANALYSIS: The zone of privacy grows smaller as scrutiny increase upon high profile black athletes that have high expectations of moral decorum placed upon them by the public. Think about how with all that is facing the nation, this event becomes a national story. Does every white celebrity tip appropriately? If not, is it worthy of *national* coverage?

Under the rubric of *power & control*, perhaps what is unstated yet nonetheless implied is that these nonwhite athletes have been granted reprieve from the Unholy Trinity in exchange for leveraging their entertaining talents, therefore, to not be a good citizen and show generosity to working whites who (at the moment) appear to be beneath this athlete on the proverbial "social food chain," is downright unbecoming. The Model Citizen should know better on how to behave in public. This is another stylized form of expressing exasperation over impudence; the nonwhite athlete must simply "know their place."

Model Citizen Example #8

Athlete (race)	Sport/ League	Situation	When
Sam Cassell (black)	NBA	Cassell was blamed by Minnesota Timberwolves coach Flip Saunders for losing 2004 NBA title.	November 2014

SOURCE: http://www.sbnation.com/nba/2014/11/4/7154423/sam-cassell-dance-flip-saunders-kevin-martin-timberwolves

BRIEF ANALYSIS: In a reflective interview a decade after the Minnesota Timberwolves lost their 2004 title run with a highly competitive squad, Saunders blamed Cassell's "Big Balls Dance" as the reason.

Model Citizen Example #9

Athlete (race)	Sport/ League	Situation	When
Justin Blackmon (black)	NFL	Blackmon was "stalked" leading up to NFL draft to ensure he would be a "good risk" for franchise.	Fall 2014

SOURCE: https://www.yahoo.com/sports/blogs/nfl-shutdown-corner/don-t-feel-bad-jameis--the-buccaneers-stalked-justin-blackmon-before-draft-232106667.html

BRIEF ANALYSIS: Model behavior is often an unspoken prerequisite for black players escaping the Unholy Trinity to be well compensated. This dynamic heightens the stakes for excellent performance both on an off the field/court. The significant sums of money involved therefore provide license to teams to be intrusive of the personal sphere since they have the right to protect their future investment of funds. Here, both Justin Blackmon and Jameis Winston were publicly spied upon and such facts were admitted openly.

NFL's Miami Dolphin's General Manager Jeff Ireland even asked Dez Bryant whether his mother was a prostitute during pre-draft interviews in 2010 (http://espn.go.com/dallas/nfl/news/story?id=5140313). It unconscionable and inconceivable to conceptualize an appropriate scenario elsewhere in corporate America for a young white female applying for a job in say, the accounting industry, to be queried over whether her mother dabbled in "evening activities for pay" as prerequisite evidence of trustworthiness for the potential accountant's employment.

Model Citizen Example #10

Athlete (race)	Sport/ League	Situation	When
Cam Newton (black)	NFL	Newton criticized via open letter to the Charlotte Observer over his touchdown celebrations.	Fall 2015

SOURCE: http://www.charlotteobserver.com/opinion/article45163665.html

BRIEF ANALYSIS: Under the rubric of *power & control,* a "concerned" white mother used her nine-year old daughter as a veil to generate sympathy while simultaneously chastising Newton for not behaving like a Model Citizen. The author attempted to utilize Negrophobia as a means to make her point. Yet, it is an open question whether she or anyone else wrote open letters (that were published! — note the decision by the mostly white-run Charlotte Observer to even publish the letter in the first place) about MLB National League Championship Series winning pitcher Madison Bumgarner setting a good example when articles appear lauding his ability to chug five beers simultaneously (http://sports. yahoo.com/blogs/mlb-big-league-stcw/madison-bumgarner-chugs-five-beers-at-once-after-giants-advance-to-nlcs-060309611.html)?[10]

Keys to the Game

- *FEATURES:* tangible display of humanity (power, dignity & respect)

- *KEY WORDS:* "no red flags," "being a team player," maturity, disciplined, "apologized"

- Adrian Peterson: Consider this Yahoo! Sports journalist's take on this event being an opportunity "to educate" others about how best to govern their behavior as well: http://sports.yahoo. com/news/roger-goodell-was-right-to-drop-hammer-on-adrian-peterson--now-nfl-needs-to-educate-152857241.html

- Consider these examples of Escape-goats, or sports individuals or institutions that did not exemplify desired behavior and therefore must be punished — University of Michigan's "Fab Five," Reggie Bush, or Terrelle Pryor. Compare to Johnny Manziel's "money sign," or celebratory gesture of rubbing his thumb against his forefingers, first exhibited against Rice University to commemorate or burlesque the fact that he was suspended for a half after the NCAA investigated him for allegedly accepting money for autographed memorabilia

- Lastly, all professional athletes face pressure to perform. With respect to the specialized pressure nonwhite athletes face, the differences in *supportive and suppressive* pressure for Model Citizen behavior adopted by the (mostly white) media voice stems from the conceptual framework that "players from an ethnic or racial group deemed undesirable must 'compensate' the majority group through superior performance. See E. Woodrow Eckard. "Anti-Irish Job Discrimination circa 1880: Evidence from Major League Baseball," Soc Sci Hist, Vol 34, No 4, Winter 2010, p. 408

COMIC RELIEF

Sportotype #5

Sportotypes					
Menace 2 Society	Diva	Intellectually Suspect	Model Citizen	Comic Relief	Buck
Sportotypes Corresponding with Unholy Trinity					
FEAR			FASCINATION		
Negrophobia	Femininity	Romantic Racialism	Negrophobia	Femininity	Romantic Racialism
Sportotypes Corresponding with Rigged Game Goals					
POWER			CONTROL		
Misread Defenses to the Unholy Trinity					
Consistency	Competition	Catharsis	Consistency	Competition	Catharsis

Playing off the Wall Ball

Sports are many things. Among them, sports are also fun! Thus, the *Comic Relief* Sportotype is the sports figure whose culture serves as the fodder for most of the jokes; typical conduct includes boisterous and improper grammar, exaggerated motions and facial expressions, and intense emotion, often in stark contrast to standardized, White, middle-class behavior. Under the rubric of *power & control*, what must remain under scrutiny is who has the ability to decide what is funny.

After all, *professional* sports are part competition and part entertainment. The games and players are literally products advertised and shopped by the owners to the paying public. In contrast to Menace 2 Society or Diva Sportotypes that may have chips on their shoulders, this athlete is highly regarded for their pleasure principle. This Comic Relief Sportotype is instructive for it shows that the various Sportotype media patterns are not mutually exclusive, meaning, it is possible for one athlete to embody or be classified as more than one Sportotype. For example, as much as athletes fitting the Diva Sportotype are demonized, many fans admire and appreciate their gesticulations and celebrations and end up imitating them in accordance witih Comic Relief principles. These athletes can simultaneously delight and displease "us" with their creativity. Think of NFL wide receivers T.O. (i.e., Terrell Owens), Chad Johnson or Joe Horn who have invented legendary and original touchdown endzone celebrations involving "props" ranging from popcorn to pom poms to sharpie pens to cameramen to orange end zone pylons to real cell phones.[2] And when "we" say "us," "we" of course are referring to "them," or mostly white male dominated sports media.[1]

They make for colorful interviews indeed!

This Comic Relief Sportotype is primarily manifested in two ways: 1) fawning over physical characteristics and 2) manifold emasculation.

HAIR GAME?

Fawning over physical characteristics comes in different forms. The psychology behind such obsession is elusive, but hints of its sourcing can be found in the *fear & fascination* dynamic we have seen from the early days of the Unholy Trinity. To this extent, Columbia University political science professor Andrew Hacker conducted an experiment with several students whereupon he asked them "how much" they would need to be properly compensated if they were to somehow magically and suddenly exchange their white skin for black skin. Monetary values ranged well into the millions.[3]

The logic of this experiment is stunning. For on one level, many whites when provided the opportunity, would decline the ability to experience life and its attendant hardships through the lens of an African American. To do so is to acknowledge the additional "friction" that the Unholy Trinity burdens upon the individual, or it is to recognize the "absence" of indirect and direct benefits, privileges and perks associated with being white.[4] In either case, the higher the number required for "compensation," the more that students recognize a disparity of experiences. It would interesting to see whether these same students would freely quote numbers as high if asked directly about how much African Americans should receive for enslavement reparations.

The irony of this representative experiment is even more stunning. Whether it is NBA Houston Rockets guard James Harden's beard, NBA Detroit Pistons forward "Big" Ben Wallace's afro or NFL

Pittsburgh Steelers Troy Polamalu long, flowing curly locks, many a fan has come to the stadium attempting to approximate the likeness of the athlete they admire and hold in high regard. In other words, many white fans do all that they can to "be black." Yet in leaving the stadium at the end of the night, most likely do not want to be black, go to the "black part of town" and live a black life. Even though many will wake up in the morning, go to their local gym with the message: "Smile, You're Darker!"[5]

The psychology behind these acts strike as either embarrassingly simple or exceedingly complicated. The simple tack has us consider that fans are just that: fanatic! Thus, it is no stretch to see that fans will seek to express their enthusiasm in a variety of creative ways.

On the other hand, when considering the larger historical context of the Unholy Trinity, such acts may possibly take on a different meaning. Online "Google searches" of "James Harden fan beard" or "Eddie Lacy chedlocks" (cheddar dredlocks for NFL Green Bay Packers running back who in addition to his wicked weight-defying spin move, is known for his signature dredlocks hairstyle) reveal diverse pictures of diverse fans imitating and emulating their diverse sports heroes. Yet, the pictures are not diverse in one aspect: virtually all of the fans depicted are white. Ergo, cultural appropriation may be at stake.

What does this mean?

In looking at the converse construct, pictures of mostly black and brown fans donning blonde wigs to imitate their favorite baseball player such as Mike Trout or Bryce Harper simply do not exist. Further, pictures of black and brown fans donning afro wigs to imitate their favorite NBA or NFL player are virtually non-existent as well. Instead, it is mostly white fans who temporarily "adopt" defining physical characteristics of black and brown players as an added level of enjoyment and entertainment for the game they love. As if they were merely adopting a costume dressing up for Halloween.[6]

Practically speaking, if a black fan already has an afro hairstyle, or frequently is exposed to such hairstyles due to personal association, perhaps the fascination factor is reduced significantly as one is already intimately familiar with the concept. Thus, it is possible that white fans who engage in such conduct may be signifying on a subconscious level an attempt to revive Romantic Racialist notions of old, whereupon blacks are highly prized, valued and revered as being superior — but only within a limited sports/entertainment context.

FUNNY HOW THE BALL BOUNCES

This Comic Relief Sportotype is the polar opposite of the Diva, where impudence was shunned. Here, such impudence is embraced to the extent it can be burlesqued, most often in the form of *emasculation*, to better put the potentially threatening nonwhite athlete "back in their place." Impudence is simply no laughing matter.

It must be reiterated that similar to the discussion on the Diva Sportotype that in critiquing emasculation, we must take care to not to conflate such commentary with criticism of effeminate manners, dress or dealings. The point is that especially for a male who publicly identifies himself and his earning potential based upon his perceived macho masculinity and in light of historical data that informs that black males were viewed and institutionally identified as the primary threat to white male supremacy, the muting of black male masculinity can be problematic indeed.

Additionally, when considering that frequently within an advertising context, nonwhite sports figures are emasculated in order to appeal to a mostly white fan base's sense of humor, such a manuever makes the nonwhite athlete less threatening and more marketable. Rippling muscles, raw power, jaw-dropping speed, ferocious drive are all admirable qualities of the nonwhite athlete — but when controlled and when not leveraged or directed at white patrons. Emasculation for entertainment allows for white patrons to take potentially foreboding presence of a nonwhite athlete that normally is superior to their stature and "bring them down to size," to a level that the average patron can access without feeling threatened.

Mike Trout can be a god. Kevin Durant can be a gutter cleaner.[7]

JUST FOR SPORT

In the ten examples that follow, consider the Unholy Trinity and how they may inform or influence coverage of the story outlined. Examples of the Comic Relief Sportotype include, but are not limited to:

Comic Relief Example #1

Athlete (race)	Sport/ League	Situation	When
Tiger Woods (black)	PGA	In wake of "the incident," the New York Post ran 21 straight stories on the situation.	December 2009

SOURCE: http://www.mediaite.com/online/tiger-woods-now-officially-more-important-than-911-in-eyes-of-new-york-post/

BRIEF ANALYSIS: Tiger's total number of consecutive cover stories for the tabloid New York Post (daily circulation @ 454,000) was greater than the total number of cover stories for September 11, 2001. Tiger's story falls under the rubric of *power & control*, in that it just happens to intersect along the lines of sex, money and power whereby a nonwhite male has sexual affairs with several "attractive" white women all the while married to another "attractive" blonde white woman while playing a game traditionally associated with the white upper class and having the power to dominate it. Some snarky titles include:

> *"Cagey Tiger"*

> *"Tiger's Back 9"*

> *"I'm A Cheetah"*

> *"Tiger's Green Fees"*

> *"Tiger's Wife Turns Tail"*

> *"Tiger Pulls Out"*

> *"Tiger's Birdies"*

Other "satirical" or humorous pieces about Tiger that take on the manifold emasculation tack include: http://sports.yahoo.com/blogs/golf-devil-ball-golf/tiger-woods-blasts-satirical-golf-digest-piece-by-legendary-dan-jenkins-205553800.html; http://www.golfdigest.com/golf-tours-news/2014-12/dan-jenkins-fake-interview-with-tiger

Comic Relief Example #2

Athlete (race)	Sport/ League	Situation	When
Manny Ramirez (Latino)	MLB	In the name of "fun," fans support their team and star player by emulating the player's physical characteristics — one's that the fan does not already have.	July 2009

SOURCE: http://articles.latimes.com/2009/jul/04/sports/sp-manny-fans4

BRIEF ANALYSIS: Manny Ramirez has long held a reputation as one of baseball's "Bad Boys" whilst he played. But after his memorable, but rocky tenure with the MLB Boston Red Sox, Manny found life again with the Los Angeles Dodgers. His new west coast fan base wanted to demonstrate their fealty and admiration for Manny by deciding to wear wigs at the ballgames consisting of fake braids that hearkened back to Manny's actual hairstyle in real life. Romantic Racialism is "at play" here.

Again, are fans merely being fans of the game? Or perhaps truly fanatical about blackness just the same (https://www.yahoo.com/news/blogs/trending-now/fan-caught-on-camera-sneaking-a-sniff-of-nba-player-164801957.html)?

Comic Relief Example #3

Athlete (race)	Sport/ League	Situation	When
Russell Westbrook (black)	NBA	Westbrook's choice in dress questioned by media.	Fall 2013

SOURCE: http://www.cbssports.com/nba/photos/10-nuttiest-outfits-russell-westbrook-wore-off-the-court

BONUS SOURCE: http://www.cbssports.com/nfl/eye-on-football/24720647/look-this-is-what-cam-newton-wore-to-his-post-game-presser

BRIEF ANALYSIS: Westbrook is but one of the more recent targets who the sports media fixates upon. In addition to receiving scrutiny for how well he reads defenses and plays defense, he now essentially has no defense to aspersions cast upon his choice of dress off the court — all in the name of good humor, of course. Perhaps a sophisticated and subtle response to the enforced NBA Dress Code, Westbrook now has his own clothing line entitled "Public School" (http://www.sportsgrid.com/nba/11-reasons-you-should-consider-buying-russell-westbrooks-new-clothing-line/).

BONUS ANALYSIS: Cam Newton has undergone similar scrutiny. Perhaps the difference is Newton states that he is fortunate to "have the swag to be able to pull it off" (http://www.foxsports.com/buzzer/story/cam-newton-says-he-fortunate-to-have-enough-swag-to-wear-foxtail-112415). Newton must "be careful" not to sound impudent with such statements.

Comic Relief Example #4

Athlete (race)	Sport/ League	Situation	When
Donovan McNabb (black)	NFL	McNabb tackled in IHOP commercial.	Fall 2009

SOURCE: https://www.youtube.com/watch?v=sDEBtoiRRBc

BRIEF ANALYSIS: For this otherwise nondescript International House of Pancakes commercial advertising "MVP Quarterback Scrambles," the main ingredient in this humorous serving is emasculation. McNabb first appears as a server taking orders from white customers but is interrupted as he is not only tackled to the floor, but is also instructed by a more diminutive white female (Rene Moran) "That's MY table McNabb!" Of note is the "goal line" camera angle from the floor that has McNabb's dazed head in the lower right-hand corner of the screen while it points upward at a triumphant and defiant Moran standing literally over McNabb as she points for emphasis. Femininity and Negrophobia strike again.

Comic Relief Example #5

Athlete (race)	Sport/ League	Situation	When
Kobe Bryant (black)	NBA	White radio announcers make fun of Kobe's deeper, black male voice.	Fall 2014

SOURCE: http://http://www.foxsportsradio.com/media/podcast-jay-mohr-sports-hours-Jay_Mohr_Sports_Hours/1211-jay-mohr-sports-hr-2-25676697/

BRIEF ANALYSIS: Start listening around the 35:10 mark of Hour 2 of the Jay Mohr Sports Show from December 11, 2014. The announcers are purposely attempting to read quotes from Bryant in the vein of a "black 36-year old male" voice to sound like Bryant. Chuckles, giggles, smirks and snarky humor ensues. No harm, no foul, no blood, no ambulance.

Again, conduct your own independent investigation to find examples of the reverse construct: a nationally syndicated black sports talk radio host of his own show reading quotes from a white athlete to sound "white."

Comic Relief Example #6

Athlete (race)	Sport/ League	Situation	When
Larry Johnson (black)	NBA	Larry Johnson gains fame, fortune and fun dunking basketballs as "Grandmama."	Fall 1993

SOURCE: https://www.youtube.com/watch?v=thbUkBW_ftM

BRIEF ANALYSIS: Cross-dressing as a grandmother, complete with floral dress and wig is not the issue. White males determining and deciding how other hyper-masculine nonwhite males will be depicted for humorous purposes is the issue. This theme of black male emasculation at their expense for white male profit is consistent with roots in the Era of Enslavement.

Additional examples include heavyweight boxing champion Evander Holyfield not only being corrected by a diminutive white female Taco Bell employee that "Even someone of your size only needs one" after "incorrectly" ordering two half-pound Nacho Crunch Burritos, but also appearing in drag posing as his own "mama" (https://www.youtube.com/watch?v=S6cBmrNbAK4) and DeAndre Jordan as "Mrs. Hooper" (complete with ill-fitting dress, heels and blonde wig) in the State Farm commercial campaign about "The Hoopers" family (https://www.youtube.com/watch?v=zrIMXZST3go). Mr. Jordan's image in this commercial is in stark contrast to the mean-mugging, high-flying dunking machine he built his early reputation upon with the NBA's Los Angeles Clippers.

Comic Relief Example #7

Athlete (race)	Sport/ League	Situation	When
Eric Striker (black)	NFL	NFL Draft prospect must answer for angry reaction to racist incident he did not find funny.	April 2016

SOURCE: http://www.mobypicture.com/user/erinasimon/view/17906456

BRIEF ANALYSIS: In March of 2015, Oklahoma University (OU) fraternity Sigma Alpha Epsilon made national headlines when members were caught on camera singing songs of a racist character (e.g., "You can hang 'em from a tree/He will never sign with me/There will never be a n*gger in SAE!"). Eric Striker was a OU football player at the time and immediately posted an emotional reaction. Striker was upset for he stated that the very same fraternity operated off of Romantic Racialist notions of comity when they invited football players to party with them and advertised that fact freely on campus. Striker did not think the SAE stunt was funny.

Yet, a year later, when attempting to position himself for the 2016 NFL Draft, Striker's honest reaction similarly is not viewed as funny, and Striker has had to "answer" for his actions and explain his views as potential NFL teams evaluate whether Striker would be a good fit. To add "insult to injury," Striker has even been billed as the "villain" (http://sportsday. dallasnews.com/college-sports/oklahomasooners/2016/03/09/qa-eric-striker-oklahoma-linebacker-still-mind-villain). "Victim" might also apply.

Comic Relief Example #8

Athlete (race)	Sport/ League	Situation	When
Cam Newton (black)	NFL	Cam Newton is directly challenged by a smaller player in a NFL PLAY 60 commercial.	November 2012

SOURCE: https://www.youtube.com/watch?v=6aKYZFcmAmU

BRIEF ANALYSIS: The NFL's *PLAY 60* campaign is designed to encourage youth to take breaks (presumptively from watching 3-hour football telecasts) and obtain at least sixty minutes of exercise daily. Here, a "cute" commercial is created when a young white male child (@ 6 to 8 years of age) asks NFL Pro Bowl quarterback and 2015 MVP Cam Newton if he wants to be his backup. Cam says "Whoa!" but the commercial ends with the kid having the "last word," with a visual of the kid repeatedly winding up his arm. The principle and theme of the commercial is generically humorous — the idea that a child has no sense of perspective while maintaining a sense of belief. Yet, seeing how there are also black child fans and (a majority of) white NFL quarterbacks, it is interesting to ponder what the reverse construct would look like, vis a vis, a small black kid asking Hall of Famer Peyton Manning to be his back up, complete with the internet responding in kind with reflexive calls for the black kids' imminent stardom, complete with over 1.6M views on YouTube.

Comic Relief Example #9

Athlete (race)	Sport/ League	Situation	When
Mike Tyson (black)	Boxing	"The Hangover, Part II" surprise closing scene when he sings "One Night in Bangkok"	May 2011

SOURCE: https://www.youtube.com/watch?v=XPMkzIwbcKs

BRIEF ANALYSIS: The rehabilitation of Menace 2 Society Tyson is complete with his emasculation/domestication. No longer a threat, white males can now manipulate his image for sport when the opposite would be true if they faced him competitively during his prime (https://www.youtube.com/watch?feature=player_embedded&v=tAB3AhpTlAw). Tyson's descent is reminiscent of late great Joe Louis and his function as a greeter in Las Vegas casinos (http://sports.jrank.org/pages/2936/Louis-Joe-Declining-Years.html).

Comic Relief Example #10

Athlete (race)	Sport/ League	Situation	When
Todd Gurley (black)	NFL	Todd Gurley in a "life sucks" campaign for the hard candy Jolly Ranchers," dons a pink tutu and sings "I'm a little teapot" during a rookie hazing ritual	Fall 2015

SOURCE: https://m.youtube.com/watch?v=xj3CzSAmzvY

BRIEF ANALYSIS: The Gurley man/girlie-man reference is clear emasculation, especially in contrast to white athletes like Brett Favre or Madison Bumgarner being framed as "men's men."

KEYS TO THE GAME

- *FEATURES*: fawning over physical, manifold emasculation

- *KEY WORDS*: ha ha, hee hee

8

BUCK

Sportotype #6

Sportotypes					
Menace 2 Society	Diva	Intellectually Suspect	Model Citizen	Comic Relief	Buck
Sportotypes Corresponding with Unholy Trinity					
FEAR			FASCINATION		
Negrophobia	Femininity	Romantic Racialism	Negrophobia	Femininity	Romantic Racialism
Sportotypes Corresponding with Rigged Game Goals					
POWER			CONTROL		
Misread Defenses to the Unholy Trinity					
Consistency	Competition	Catharsis	Consistency	Competition	Catharsis

PLAYING WITH BIG BALLS

The *Buck* Sportotype is the sports figure who is regarded for their physical or sexual prowess, typically at the sacrifice of intellectual or emotional capacities. Defining characteristics include: 1) obsession over physical features/performance and 2) animalated expressions.

An athlete's body is a vital instrument for playing the game. Criticism of mainstream media for merely recognizing the primacy of the athlete's body would be misplaced. Yet, the athlete is more than their mere body. The body is the vehicle by which human thought, emotion and feeling are expressed. After all, any Winter Olympics telecast will readily inform the viewer that the participating (American) athletes are more than mere competitors. They are people with personal identities and ideas. The reason why we know so much is because such telecasts tell us so much with their in-depth profiles and backstories created for viewer contextualization. Many Americans may already be predisposed to root for American competitors, but upon learning how humble and hard the amateur speed skater's path to glory has been, a larger emotional connection is made making every effort towards victory onscreen all the more meaningful.

Unfortunately, many nonwhite athletes within the world of basketball and football do not benefit from such in-depth coverage and instead we see an heightened emphasis placed upon their bodies. Literally. For instance, take this description of a black male high school running back standout under the heading "First and 10: Physical Freaks": "[Derrius] Guice stands out at a *rock solid* 5-foot-11 and 215 pounds. He has a *stout build* and he has the ability to *intimidate* as soon as he steps off the bus. He already has a *college build* and the *strength* to go along with it. From his *barrel chest* to his *powerful legs,* Guice is easy to spot in a crowd"[1] (emphasis added). The words in bold highlight the fascination with this young black male's body, complete with descriptors seldom seen in white-dominated baseball, hockey, tennis, golf or volleyball scouting reports.

WHIPPING UP THE PAST

Perhaps nowhere is the lurid fascination of the black body, its value and performance highlighted greater than during the annual NFL Combine that takes place in Indianapolis, Indiana following the Super Bowl in February. Here, more than 300 players have the opportunity to showcase their physical attributes in advance of the impending NFL draft in April. Many of the invited prospects have already amassed at least two years' worth of "film," or footage of them performing spectacularly, so the task at the combine is to verify that the superhuman glimpsed on film is indeed real in the flesh. Thus measurements are taken, physiques are scrutinized and bodies are tested — all in the name of due diligence by NFL franchises that wish not to make a foolhardy investment and waste limited draft picks.

Part of the due diligence includes asking players to "strip down" to mere undergarments in order to ensure that potential employees "look the part."[2] While professional players from the four major sports are all vetted before being placed upon a roster, the question remains whether MLB and NHL testing matches up with such NFL tactics. If not, then what are the possible implications? While the NFL Combine undoubtedly includes white players, the data illustrates that the majority of players undergoing this process are black. Does then, the idea of black bodies scrutinized upon a public platform for potential bidders wishing to leverage the labor of the black body for personal profit of a white owner sound familiar? If so, familiar to what?

To not "hide the ball" any further, some have suggested that the aforedescribed dynamic is reminiscent of *slavery,* otherwise known as the "third rail" of sports media.[3] To be clear, the NFL Combine is not slavery. Individuals voluntarily participate and while whipped into shape, no one is certainly whipped. Further, some of these players harbor the potential to become handsomely compensated for their services, something that never happened during the Era of Enslavement. If anything, now that the paychecks have increased, more scrutiny is placed upon player performance in evaluating whether the athlete represents a good investment and can provide an adequate return.

For example, the NBA in 2014 proposed technology described as "CARFAX for the athlete," whereby players would wear devices measuring heart rates and caloric exertion during play.[4] Such new technology requires players wear small GPS devices inside the back of their jerseys between their shoulder blades to better record every move a player makes (beware to the player that deigns to "take plays off"). It would stand to reason that franchises would analyze the information under the auspices of becoming an informed consumer. Such intrusive measurements are justified with economic logic:

> Given how *costly* injuries to key contributors can prove to both on-court success (in terms of wins losses) and off-court *bottom lines* (in terms of *gate receipts* and *merchandise sales*), it stands to reason that organizations would have a vested interest in doing just about anything within their power to protect those *investments* by keeping players in *sound enough working order* to remain on the court as much as possible.[5] (emphasis added)

This logic is all fine and good. The question is whether we see such logic consistently applied to white dominated sports as well.[6]

The thread of continuity at stake here is the *power & control* dynamic from earlier times wherein blacks were valued primarily only for their bodies. Thus, the Buck Sportotype poses age-old questions of ownership regarding "who's body is it?" and "who's work product is it?" Are most Americans subjected to similar scrutiny regarding "hustle stats" kept on their person to ensure that every waking minute on the job is used efficiently in the name of company production?[7]

While this manuscript does not advance that professional sports are akin to slavery, some parallels are striking. Particularly in the NFL and NBA, the best bodies are coveted based upon the advantages they present in physical, contact-based sports. A quick look at the NFL combine will reflect this fascination. Half naked[8] black bodies are regarded almost as specimens while mostly white males marvel at their incredible physiques, knowing that they can never create, build or live in such a body, but have the opportunity to "brand" the body with the logo of their franchise, claiming ownership, or *power & control* over the body's total work product.

Finally, author William Rhoden (*Forty Million Dollar Slaves*) suggests that despite the fact that such labor appears to be well compensated, a complex, institutionalized "conveyor belt" machinery continues to exploit disadvantaged black labor, starting from childhood. After all, most black NBA players do not hail from Beverly Hills or Martha's Vineyard. To Rhoden's point, Dale Brown, a famous and beloved elderly white male basketball coach at Louisiana State University once stated: "Look at the money we make off predominantly poor black kids...We're the whoremasters."[9] What we find worthy of further critical analysis is to what degree the power dynamic between endowed and empowered whites[10] and mendicant and marginalized blacks has changed from slavery to present. While formerly impoverished black players should indeed be grateful to receive millions to merely "play a game," what often escapes scrutiny is the lone individual who can afford to pay more than fifty players tens of millions of dollars apiece. This white male has infinitely more power than the black player who is only as good as his last play.

BEAST MODE

In emphasizing the physical body[11] at the expense of one's humanity, it is important to also keep an eye out for animal references commonly made with nonwhite athletes. Whereas it is common for members of the media to rave about the build and ability of an athlete, white athletes are often humanized, while black athletes are often animalized.

Animalization occurs with direct references to the athlete being "like a beast," "strong as a horse/ox," "as fast as a cheetah," etc. Such references to "freakish athleticism" and "natural talent" for white players are seldom since many are portrayed as having "worked hard" to cultivate whatever *skills and techniques* they have. This subtle, yet subconscious shift presupposes a Romantic Racialist narrative that blacks are naturally gifted in the body, which thereby "explains" their superiority rather than consider the mathematical possibility that the black athlete simply outworked or outthought their white competition.

Additionally, the subtle association of black athletes with "primal," or savage qualities is frequently seen in the realm of basketball, whereupon players are often depicted frozen in time with their mouths open in a screaming fashion, complete with neck veins bulging. Such expressions are indeed emoted typically follow an impressive dunk or incredibly difficult or important play during the game. Yet, given the vast array of choices media editors have, look for yourself to see just how often black players are frozen in time emoting despite there being a plethora of other shots featuring the player "looking normal."

Editors will likely argue that such emotion was important to capture and helped communicate the essence of the storyline without having to use additional text. Fine. But MLB players emote after strike outs and homeruns as well. Compare leading story photos for yourself.

JUST FOR SPORT

In the ten examples that follow, consider the Unholy Trinity and how they may inform or influence coverage of the story outlined. Examples of the Buck Sportotype include, but are not limited to:

Buck Example #1

Athlete (race)	Sport/ League	Situation	When
Tiger Woods (black)	PGA	Before "the incident," part of the fear of Mr. Woods came from the fact that he was deemed to be more physically fit than average.	November 2014

SOURCE: http://www.sbnation.com/golf/2014/1/28/5352922/tiger-woods-swing-teacher-hank-haney-sean-foley-brandel-chamblee

BRIEF ANALYSIS: Woods' hulking power only had but so much sway as critics would note how far Woods could drive the ball, but the question was whether he was accurate, or whether he had he finesse to perform chip shots, wedge shots and putts as effectively too.

Buck Example #2

Athlete (race)	Sport/ League	Situation	When
Trent Williamson (black)	NFL	Upon being drafted, NFL Commissioner Roger Goodell calls Williamson by his nickname "Silverback."	April 2010

SOURCE: https://www.youtube.com/watch?v=XwqpsFI_JQY

BRIEF ANALYSIS: Dating back to times of old, black people within America have constantly battled mainstream associations with animals. Here, Williamson somehow acquired the nickname "Silverback," which refers to the alpha male, largest gorilla in a group often demarcated by a line of silver white hair running down its back. Goodell then gave the animal association legitimacy by reading it in front of a national television audience. Williamson's apparent acceptance of the nickname as an individual does not take away from the problematic nature of the nickname from an institutional standpoint.

Some athletes play into this trope by racing animals, likely in an attempt to demonstrate their prowess and leverage higher compensation as a result (e.g., Chad Johnson vs. horse, https://www.youtube.com/watch?v=VWGoSc28B1M; Dennis Northcutt vs. ostrich, https://www.youtube.com/watch?v=2WcMRpozO4s). For older black athletes like Jesse Owens, he took to racing horses as a way to make a living since the Amateur Athletic Union banned him for life, just weeks after his historic four gold medal run at the 1936 Berlin Olympics (http://articles.latimes.com/1986-04-20/sports/sp-1172_1_jesse-owens).

Regardless, black athletes themselves still suffer from direct animal associations as if it were normal. Imagine the following comments being made during an Olympic Beach Volleyball telecast: "I think he's a bell cow. He's a big guy, and he's physical," from Sam Gash, the Green Bay Packers running backs coach on Eddie Lacy (http://www.sbnation.com/nfl/2014/8/28/6075955/michael-vick-riley-cooper-philadelphia-eagles-eddie-lacy-packers) or "He's a workhorse. We need him in the winter months," said Packers quarterback Aaron Rodgers (http://news.yahoo.com/lacy-packers-power-past-vikings-24-21-211123828--spt.html).

Buck Example #3

Athlete (race)	Sport/ League	Situation	When
Derrick Rose (black)	NBA	Rose is literally depicted as a "bull" evading matadors before "roses" are thrown at his feet after dunking victoriously.	October 2011

SOURCE: www.youtube.com/watch?v=A1YwYSHMgaA

BRIEF ANALYSIS: Former MVP Derrick Rose played for the Chicago Bulls at the time. Not to be bullish, but get it?

Buck Example #4

Athlete (race)	Sport/ League	Situation	When
	NBA	NBA teams seek new technology to leverage optimal product performance.	October 2014

SOURCE: http://sports.yahoo.com/blogs/nba-ball-dont-lie/has-the-nba-s-biometric-data-tracking-boom-gone-too-far-070039861.html

BRIEF ANALYSIS: Consider this article quote: "the scope of this monitoring is expanding, and faster than the public knows. Teams have always intuited that on-court productivity could be undermined by off-court choices — how a player exhausts himself after hours, for instance, or what he eats and drinks. Now the race is on to comprehensively surveil and quantify that behavior. NBA executives have discovered how to leverage new, ever-shrinking technologies to supervise a player's sleeping habits, record his physical movements, appraise his diet and test his blood. In automotive terms, the league is investing in a more accurate odometer." Again, it is difficult to imagine this same level of scrutiny applied to middle and upper class white Americans who are presumed to have enough autonomy to know when and how to perform professionally without direct intrusion into their sleeping habits as a function of corporate production.

Buck Example #5

Athlete (race)	Sport/ League	Situation	When
Serena Williams (black)	USTA	Serena Williams' excellence on the tennis court is unparalleled; although winning on the court, she is not courted by advertisers.	September 2015

SOURCE: http://madamenoire.com/585085/serena-williams-deemed-greatest-athlete-time-endorsements-say-otherwise/

BRIEF ANALYSIS: If there was a hierarchy, darker skinned, non-white athletes do not even have the "privilege" of being objectified as desirable or attractive based upon their physical appearance. For whatever it's worth, despite having lost repeatedly to Williams, and only having won a fraction of Major tennis tournaments than Williams, Maria Sharapova out earns

Williams in endorsements by a mile. We must at least ask, "Is race a factor? If so, how much a factor?" For the record, Sharapova is a white female with blond hair. Why do marketers find her more marketable (https://www.yahoo.com/beauty/maria-sharapova-talks-beauty-business-vodka-102617417323.html)? Lindsey Vonn, Rhonda Rousey and Danica Patrick similarly benefit from non-athletic endorsement deals.

It is a fact that Serena and her sister Venus have endured racism from intemperate fans over the years (http://www.theroot.com/articles/culture/2014/10/insulting_venus_and_serena_isn_t_anything_new.html). When considering the focus of this article (even in defeat), we must also consider whether the Williams' sisters have also endured inconsistent treatment from the media as well (https://www.yahoo.com/news/sharapova-humbled-gracious-latest-loss-williams-140438479.html).

Buck Example #6

Athlete (race)	Sport/ League	Situation	When
Jadeveon Clowney	NFL	High expectation of high (black) performance for high draft pick — even through injury.	February 2014

SOURCE: http://sports.yahoo.com/blogs/ncaaf-dr-saturday/steve-spurrier-calls-jadeveon-clowney-ethic-ok-170533822--ncaaf.html

BRIEF ANALYSIS: Clowney's college football coach, University of South Carolina' Steve Spurrier, gave a lukewarm endorsement of his star player before the NFL Draft that "raised questions about Clowney's durability and his willingness to play through injury – a red flag for a lot of NFL scouts." The pressure for black male athletes to "prove their worth" by playing through injury is concerning in view of data showing NFL players sustained more than 30,000 injuries in the ten-year period from 2002-2011 (http://www.washingtonpost.com/sf/feature/wp/2013/05/16/do-no-harm-retired-nfl-players-endure-a-lifetime-of-hurt/)

This pressure to perform is a one-way street, meaning under the rubric of *power & control*, it is virtually unheard of to see a nonwhite male: a) in a postition of undisputed authority over another white male and b) exercise such authority to publicly chastise the white male over matters that likely could also be expressed privately. Compare Indianapolis Colts' Chuck Pagano's "losing patience" with injured veterans since "it's time for them to get on the field and start "playing football" (http://sports.yahoo.com/news/richardson-tries-next-step-colts-164917098--nfl.html) with MLB's Chicago Cubs Jake Arrieta not having to pitch due to a blister on his thumb (http://wgntv.com/2016/03/24/thumb-blister-forces-jake-arrieta-out-of-the-cubs-game-against-the-giants/).

Buck Example #7

Athlete (race)	Sport/ League	Situation	When
	NFL	Dog collars issued to players who play "ferocious" defense	October 2014

SOURCE: http://www.clevelandbrowns.com/news/article-1/Culture-Change-Browns-implement-dog-collars-to-strengthen-the-defense--/c62c5d6b-07a6-4a8d-a595-d1a5d413a91d

BRIEF ANALYSIS: White Defensive Coordinator Jim O'Neil issues dog collars to mostly black players who excel on defense. The article photo may be distracting as a black male player holds up the dog collars with pride. The players' pride notwithstanding, the difference between "colleague" and "collared" are nonetheless significant.

Buck Example #8

Athlete (race)	Sport/ League	Situation	When
Carmelita Jeter & Justin Gatlin (black)	USTF	Cheetahs named after black Olympic athletes as an honor to their speedy achievements on the track.	July 2012

SOURCE: http://nationalzoo.si.edu/Animals/AfricanSavanna/News/cheetahcubs2012.cfm

BRIEF ANALYSIS: Before deciding whether Example #8 is "too sensitive," consider how a Japanese zoo apologized for naming a monkey "Charlotte," after the British Princess born in early 2015. "Many critics said giving the princess' name to a monkey was disrespectful to British royals" (http://news.yahoo.com/japan-zoo-apologizes-naming-newborn-monkey-charlotte-084607045.html), although the "decision to name the cubs after the fastest Americans is part of a broader National Zoo Games campaign to celebrate the Zoo's finest animaletes."

Buck Example #9

Athlete (race)	Sport/ League	Situation	When
Michael Crabtree (black)	NFL	Financial evaluation analysis continues of black male athletes and their worth.	October 2009

SOURCE: http://content.usatoday.com/communities/thehuddle/
post/2009/10/will-the-49ers-get-anything-useful-out-of-michael-crabtree-
before-2010/1

BRIEF ANALYSIS: The article title, "Will the [San Francisco] 49ers Get Anything Useful out of Michael Crabtree before 2010?" reads a bit dismissive about Crabtree's humanity; people speak with more care in evaluating their tire treads. Similar complaints are hard to find for white players. Research and investigate the flameout failure of rare NFL white running back Peyton Hillis, or MLB's Brian Wilson.

Buck Example #10

Athlete (race)	Sport/ League	Situation	When
	NFL	NFL Draft prospect asked to take off shirt and pose.	March 2009

SOURCE: http://www.outsports.com/2009/3/11/4047346/nfl-draft-
prospect-asked-to-pose-shirtless

BRIEF ANALYSIS: Is a similar process necessary or necessarily employed for the U.S. Women's Soccer tryouts?

KEYS TO THE GAME

- KEY WORDS: workhorse, natural, athletic (but isn't everyone who plays a sport "athletic"?), specimen, freakish athlete, horse, beast

- TAME THE BEAST: http://sports.yahoo.com/news/u-s--s-big-challenge-against-belgium--tame-the--beast-163155446.html

INSIDE THE WHITE LINES

How Are White Athletes Scored & Judged?

PLAYING EXCEPTIONAL BALL

In any competitive competition, individuals and teams must alternately play both offense and defense — one attempts to advance their agenda and score while frustrating the aim of their opponent. If the prior analysis of the six Sportotypes represents that which is "offensive" about common patterns for nonwhite sports figures as they relate to "Race & Sports," then we should not get "defensive" about considering common patterns for white sports figures as well.

Quite simply, the overwhelming majority of white sports figures fall within one of six patterns entitled *pro-totypes* which humanize or glamorize their participation above and beyond the game in contrast to Sportotypes that marginalize nonwhite participation. These patterns evidence *faith & facilitation* in the white player and their abilities:

White Pro-totype Sports Figures	
Affluent	Net worth, not salary, described to prove this figure's value; think "owner"
Family-Tied	Connected to a traditional family legacy the audience respects; think of the Manning NFL football family
The Hero	Has a personal narrative that the audience understands as a driving force, a larger cause that justifies support; think Lance Armstrong's "Livestrong" campaign
The Intellectual	Displays incredible acumen in playing or approaching the game; think Tom Brady or Aaron Rodgers and what is said about their preparations and earned successes
The Manipulator	Leverages their skill set to the maximum, often when challenged in normally overwhelming competitive circumstances; think Steve Nash or Wes Welker as "undersized white boys" who "fearlessly compete"
The Romantic	Has finesse that extends beyond the game as reflected by their attractive paramours; such paramours typically fulfill the White Beauty Standard and are frequently displayed at the end of important games

It is not to say that nonwhite sports figures are *never* depicted within a familial or romantic setting. It is to say that white athletes are showcased along the Pro-totypes much more consistently within mainstream media along the two poles of *faith & facilitation* as opposed to the *fear & fascination* poles consistent with nonwhite athlete Sportotypes.

WANNA PLAY A GAME?

Studying nonwhites and whites in isolation from one another is the equivalent to a coach scheduling practices but never scheduling games against live competition. Plays may be executed to perfection during imaginary walk-throughs, but coach can only confidently say they have evaluated the team once the players actually had to play "for keeps." It follows, we will briefly analyze ten examples that juxtapose white and nonwhite sports figures to see whether marginalization or glamorization is truly happening under the more intense scrutiny of instant replay. The game is entitled *Apples 2 Oranges* whereupon two sports figures will be paired with similarities (apples) and differences (oranges) within a common theme. Using our principle of *Just Add Water*, perform your own analysis to see whether the two sports figures of two different races received consistent treatment, all things considered, and if not, whether race was a factor for the difference.

Apples 2 Oranges Example #1	
Sports Figures	Bruce Pearl vs. Nolan Richardson
Apples (same)	Both males, NCAA Division I head coaches, had conflict with their employing universities
Oranges (different)	Richardson = black male, has never served as head coach in NCAA since; Pearl = white male, back as NCAA D-I head coach within three years

SOURCES:>https://sports.yahoo.com/wnba/news?slug=dw-richardson051710
>http://espn.go.com/mens-college-basketball/story/_/id/10626778/bruce-pearl-accepts-auburn-tigers-head-basketball-coaching-job

BRIEF ANALYSIS: These two coaches help flesh out the *marginality theory* that nonwhites have a smaller margin of error, but a greater margin of punishment. Richardson, despite winning a D-I national championship and going to the tournament 13 times in 17 years, was summarily fired after openly complaining after one game. Pearl, never won a D-I championship and was found to have lied in violation of NCAA rules and encouraged others to lie.

Pearl along with several other white males in power, demonstrate that when they fall from grace, their castigation is often temporary and malleable; rehabilitation is always possible. Sean Payton, Dave Bliss, Steve Masiello, Bobby Petrino and Rick Pitino are but a few.[1]

Apples 2 Oranges Example #2	
Sports Figures	Marcus Mariota vs. Jameis Winston
Apples (same)	Both males, NFL Draft first round picks, both started for their NFL teams on opening day
Oranges (different)	Winston lost his debut while Mariota won; difference in media pressure emerged (supportive vs. suppressive)
SOURCES: >http://sports.yahoo.com/blogs/nfl-shutdown-corner/perfect-marcus-mariota-outplays-inept-jameis-winston-in-their-debuts-231151931.html >www.csnne.com/new-england-patriots/esiason-i-didnt-realize-how-far-away-winston	

BRIEF ANALYSIS: Mariota is of Samoan descent on his father's side, his mother's side is German. While Mariota is not fully "white" in ethnic identity, this example is nonetheless instructive of how *suppressive pressure versus supportive pressure* works. Winston is classified as "inept" in his first game ever as a NFL starter, whereas in the same article, it is difficult to determine whether Mariota is already in the Hall of Fame based upon the praise.

The level of scrutiny black quarterback Winston endures is not common with all quarterbacks; Carson Wentz has "seemingly come out of nowhere," and escaped heavy media scrutiny leading up to the 2016 NFL Draft despite not playing at a nationally known school or winning a D-I national championship as evidence of skill or go undefeated the way Winston did (http://www.businessinsider.com/carson-wentz-pro-day-throw-2016-3).

Apples 2 Oranges Example #3

Sports Figures	Andy Moeller vs. Ray Farmer
Apples (same)	Both males, affiliated with NFL team Cleveland Browns in professional working capacity, both made mistakes eventually leading to their loss of jobs
Oranges (different)	Farmer = black male, serves as General Manager, was suspended four games and team fined $250,000 for his transgression; Moeller = white male, offensive line coach not arrested, team initially suspended him indefinitely

SOURCE: >http://profootballtalk.nbcsports.com/2015/09/07/browns-ol-coach-was-not-arrested-police-will-share-more-tuesday/

>http://www.nfl.com/news/story/0ap3000000482496/article/browns-gm-ray-farmer-suspended-4-games-for-texting

BONUS SOURCE: http://nypost.com/2015/07/13/bills-coach-gave-boy-a-black-eye-in-beach-punchout-cops/

BRIEF ANALYSIS: Farmer was found guilty of sending text messages to coaches and Browns personnel during the game in violation of policies designed to prevent any unfair competitive advantage. The league, presumably to protect the integrity of its product, stepped in and disciplined the team regardless of what punishment the team would decide. In contrast, Moeller was the subject of an investigation after his fiancee alleged he physically assaulted her in September, 2015. The local prosecutor declined to press charges although he stated "it is quite clear an incident of volatile nature took place," the team initially suspended Moeller and then the two parties "mutually agreed to part ways," rather than the Browns expressly terminate Moeller for detrimental conduct, especially in light of a renewed emphasis on domestic violence prevention courtesy of the Ray Rice incident awareness. Moeller demonstrates the plasticity of criminality many white males experience as he was found guilty of DUI in 2011 only after his third alcohol-related arrest in four years — and still was able to keep his job with...the Baltimore Ravens at the time!

BONUS ANALYSIS: In July of 2015, offensive line coach Aaron Kromer punched a teenage boy "in the face and threatened to kill his family in a dispute over beach chairs." Kromer was suspended, but did not lose his job in this non-domestic, but violent incident; the Florida state attorney's office dropped misdemeanor battery charges against Kromer leaving him free to resume his coaching life.

Apples 2 Oranges Example #4

Sports Figures	Ray Rice vs. Ravens cheerleader
Apples (same)	Both affiliated with NFL's Baltimore Ravens in professional working capacity, both engaged in reprehensive behavior towards another person
Oranges (different)	Rice = black male, Ravens running back struck his wife in an elevator, became national symbol of domestic violence; Shattuck = white female, Ravens cheerleader, avoided both jail time and public scrutiny despite raping a 15-year old boy

SOURCES: >http://www.usatoday.com/story/sports/nfl/ravens/2015/02/13/ray-rice-apologizes-to-baltimore-ravens-fans-in-a-statement/23344331/ >http://www.usatoday.com/story/sports/nfl/2015/08/21/molly-shattuck-ravens-cheerleader-sentenced-rape-boy/32108039/

BRIEF ANALYSIS: This entry is not about exonerating Mr. Rice. This example merely raises the question of why Shattuck was not included in the national discussion about intimate violence and its prevention seeing how she worked for the same team and had her case processed the same time.

Apples 2 Oranges Example #5

Sports Figures	Dante Culpepper vs. Rob Gronkowski
Apples (same)	Both males, NFL football players who leveraged their celebrity for a "good time" on seafaring vessels
Oranges (different)	Culpepper = black male, suffered media maelstrom about "poor judgment" for "love boat"; Gronkowski = white male, celebrated for "party ship"

SOURCES: > http://usatoday30.usatoday.com/sports/football/nfl/vikings/2005-12-15-boat-party-charges_x.htm > http://www.gronkspartyship.com

BRIEF ANALYSIS: Culpepper in 2005 went out on a "party boat" with several teammates, several members of the opposite sex and several libations. Imaginations can speculate what happened next. A national media scandal entitled the "love boat" scandal and criminal charges for Culpepper. Fast forwarding a decade, Gronkowski is offering a "service" to the public, teammates and members of the opposite sex who also wish to have libations and a "good time." Not to rock the boat any further, yet it is unknown whether the "party ship" is also damaging to nine year old children.[2]

Apples 2 Oranges Example #6

Sports Figures	Marion Jones vs. Lance Armstrong
Apples (same)	Both are elite level athletes, were both busted for lying to doping authorities in their sport, both stripped of their titles
Oranges (different)	Jones = black female, did jail time despite being young mother; Armstrong = white male, on denial tour, kept medals, defended "it's for a good cause."

SOURCES: >http://www.cnn.com/2008/CRIME/01/11/jones.doping/
>http://news.yahoo.com/blogs/the-turnstile/livestrong-would-welcome·
back-lance-armstrong-even-now-204641190.htm

BRIEF ANALYSIS: Both Jones and Armstrong could not live a lie; Jones was ensared in a performance enhancing outfit named BALCO while Armstrong may have masterminded his own ring. Jones did jail time while Armstrong did not. Armstrong also built up a massive campaign around cancer awareness (i.e., Livestrong) that captivated the imaginations of millions of Americans. Arguably, Armstrong's falsehoods affected more people, yet his doping scandal does not generate much press as say a "decision" made by a basketball player on where to take his talents.

Apples 2 Oranges Example #7

Sports Figures	Brandon Marshall vs. Peyton Manning
Apples (same)	Both males, NFL football players, both grew exercised during game play and let their teammates know about their displeasure
Oranges (different)	Marshall = black male, was ridiculed by media for his locker room outburst; Manning = white male, anger was symbolic display of his "seriousness" and "commitment to the game."

SOURCES: >http://https://www.yahoo.com/sports/blogs/nfl-shutdown-corner/bears-locker-room-reportedly-turns-ugly-after-home-loss-to-dolphins-210405292.html
>http://sports.yahoo.com/blogs/nfl-shutdown-corner/peyton-manning--insanely-competitive--chews-out-julius-thomas-231820757.html

BRIEF ANALYSIS: It is no surprise that within an enterprise that involves literally a person's blood, sweat and tears, that emotions may become involved. Anger is not new; it is a natural human emotion. Except for when emoted by nonwhite males. Compare the criticism of Marshall

— even though he was emoting in "private," behind closed locker room doors — to other public displays of white male emotion, whether it be the destruction of computer tablets on the sideline (https://www.youtube.com/watch?v=lIXQy8V-9po), the use of profane vernacular at least seventy-seven times within an interview (http://sports.yahoo.com/blogs/mlb-big-league-stew/reds-manager-bryan-price-unleashes-77-f-bombs-in-tirade-against-local-media-024241931.html), or the destruction of computer tablets on the sideline (https://www.youtube.com/watch?v=i-clnYllFas).

Most often, white male athletes have the time and space to not only get upset, but also to display such anger without fear of severe retribution or punishment. Under the rubric of *power & control*, the subtle significant message is that nonwhite athletes are free to behave, or else face the consequences of being labeled as a Menace 2 Society rather than a Model Citizen.

Meanwhile, white athletes have a greater margin of error and a smaller margin of punishment (see 1. http://sports.yahoo.com/blogs/mlb-big-league-stew/chris-sale-pummels-unfortunate-cooler-rough-outing-against-205727128.html; 2. http://sports.yahoo.com/news/papelbon-blows-save-phils-lose-213150762--mlb.html; 3. http://sports.yahoo.com/blogs/nbc-yahoo-sports/mad-dash--scuba-diver-retrieves-rory-mcilroy-s-3-iron-152619134.html).

Apples 2 Oranges Example #8	
Sports Figures	Vince Young vs. Tim Tebow
Apples (same)	Both males, achieved significantly at the NCAA Division I level for football, had spotty careers in the NFL
Oranges (different)	Young = black male, played for more years in the league, once out of football has not been seen; Tebow = white male, intensely marketable off football field, included in national showcases
SOURCES: > http://bigstory.ap.org/article/qb-young-out-game-and-out-money >http://sports.yahoo.com/news/tim-tebow-joining-abcs-gma-204811368--nfl.html	

BRIEF ANALYSIS: Both athletes played the quarterback position and won national championships at the college level. Both faced questions about their mechanics and delivery thereby truncating their time in the league. Yet, this example highlights how much more "flammable" white personalities can be for marketing purposes as Young is washed out of the game entirely, while Tebow is not just good for football, but Hall of Flame players are calling Tebow good for our country (http://www. cnsnews.com/blog/michael-morris/mike-ditka-guys-tim-tebow-are-good-sports-good-football-good-our-country?ref=yfp)!

Tebow's celebrity, including his overt Christianity and signature touchdown celebration of appearing to kneel in "prayer" Christian players who kneel (Tebow) was indeed controversial, but one thing it was not, was penalized by NFL referees (http://sports.yahoo.com/blogs/nfl-shutdown-corner/chiefs-player-gets-penalized-after-kneeling-in-muslim-prayer-035223137.html).

Tebow's signature good looks and appeal to a majority white viewing audience that still provides him with a space to excel, despite having a pedestrian career.

Apples 2 Oranges Example #9

Sports Figures	Byron Scott vs. Brett Brown
Apples (same)	Both males, NBA head coaches
Oranges (different)	Scott = black male, was fired; Brown = white male, was rehired, has backing of management despite colossal team futility

SOURCES: > http://espn.go.com/nba/news/story?id=1718853
> http://sports.yahoo.com/news/sources--76ers-coach-brett-brown-agrees-to-two-year-extension-211004766.html

BRIEF ANALYSIS: Despite taking the New Jersey Nets to the NBA Finals twice within three years of first taking on the job, management terminated Scott despite his team leading its division, the next year after reaching the Finals the two prior years consecutively. On the contrary, Brown has "bought in" to the Philadelphia 76ers long-term rebuilding plan and has "endured two-plus years of a gutted roster, saddled with a 38-149 record."

Poor Mr. Brown.

Apples 2 Oranges Example #10	
Sports Figures	Steve Nash vs. Brandon Marshall
Apples (same)	Both males, played professional sports at elite level, both used social media to respond to intemperate fans they felt crossed the line
Oranges (different)	Marshall = black male, was criticized for being immature; Nash = white male, praised as sticking up for himself
SOURCES: >http://www.chicagotribune.com/sports/football/bears/chi-brandon-marshall-detroit-fan-20141114-column.html	
> http://www.sbnation.com/lookit/2015/2/24/8104011/steve-nash-tells-angry-tweeter-to-meet-him-in-temecula	

BRIEF ANALYSIS: This scenario allows another glimpse into the rubric of *power & control*, wherein Marshall received suppressive pressure for offering to fight a "fan" who insulted Marshall's mother on social media. Meanwhile, former NBA MVP Nash receives adulation and praise for being "badass" in his offer to meet an online troll and set him straight.

LET'S TAKE A SECOND FOR THE LADIES

Women are at a disadvantage relative to men, for in addition to their performance, they are also scrutinized for their appearance. For example, notice how the female athletes are sexualized in this restaurant advertisement, unlike an Aaron Rodgers or Peyton Manning who appear clothed and "serious" in insurance commercials: (e.g., https://www.youtube.com/watch?v=dARPOq5VPPA).

Yet, complicating our work here is the intersectionality of sexuality and race. A word about sexuality: the unique dynamic white women have as colloquially referred to as *home court/field advantage*, whereby while suppressed and subjugated relative to white men (e.g., http://sports.yahoo.com/news/jags--poolside-scene-turning-more-heads-than-football-team-021159184-nfl.html), white women nonetheless enjoy a privileged position in relation to virtually all other racial/gender demographics by virtue of their special "in-house" relationship with white men as the mothers, daughters, wives, etc. of white men. Thus, while we may not think of it this way, white women are frequently the *direct beneficiaries and targets* of white male prowess and consequently are uniquely positioned to leverage their privileged status for equality with other white men.

Also recall our earlier understandings of the "rigged game" and numerous schools of thought about how best to exclude blacks from full participation in the competitive game for limited resources. With this dynamic, white men have historically demonstrated an extreme reluctance to be beholden to or subordinate to black male masculinity. If anything, white males have demonstrated a desire to mute black male sexuality and power in the presence of white males. When white males make an exception to their masculinity being usurped, this is typically when they allow themselves self-deprecation in the presence of (usually, more attractive) white women. Think of the Chevy Silverado commercial with the ESPN Gameday Crew and Samantha Ponder.[3]

It is not surprising that whenever we see a "first" with respect to women in sports (or more specifically, women in traditionally white-male dominated enclaves within sports), it is "just happens" to be a white woman. We must be careful, for within these contexts described herein this chapter, "women" actually becomes a coded euphemism for "white women," for that is who practically has such access to such power and who the power structure has a vested interest in placating. White men in power, even if only acting out of their own self interest, realize that it is not feasibly sustainable for them to be dominant and exclusive in all professional affairs, when white women are included within their personal affairs in so many ways. The question then becomes what incentive exists for white males in power to make such accommodations for those outside of their inner circle — especially among race and gender lines. Again, we are merely being rational here, not "racist."

Yes, white women write exhaustively about being suppressed, subjugated and thought of second when it comes to their interactions with white men. Yet, many ironically benefit from their very relationships with white males that they critique. White women are also the mothers, grandmothers, sisters, daughters, aunts, nieces, wives and mistresses of white males which despite their subordinate state relative to white males, nonetheless positions them differently and accords them significant status and privilege above other groups. Observe the pattern "at play" with these links below; while second to white men, white women indeed are often thought of first:

http://sports.yahoo.com/news/nfl-hires-sarah-thomas-1st-female-official-142522519--nfl.html

http://sports.yahoo.com/blogs/mlb-big-league-stew/a-s-hire-justine-siegal--making-her-the-first-female-coach-for-an-mlb-team-222835376.html

https://www.yahoo.com/style/jen-welter-becomes-first-female-nfl-coach-125255812243.html

---

Keys to the Game

- FEATURES: a key question to ask is, how consistent are fans and media employees in applying the same criteria and scrutiny to both white and nonwhite athletes alike?

TALLYING THE FINAL SCORE

The Bottom Line on the Bottom Dime

BALL OUT OF BOUNDS

The title of this section is quite clever for while we have been having a ball thus far, it is indeed is time to take the ball out of bounds, past what we know to be normal in order to critically question the meaning of the relationship between race and sports as we tally our final score. By way of recall, we are able to bring to the forefront what had been in the back of our minds throughout this text; namely that there was a rebuttable presumption we sought to explore: "*There is NO racism in American sport*":

Rebuttable Presumption
"*There is NO racism in American sport*"
1.   sports are a meritocracy
2.   due to emphasis on results and not "color," many non-white athletes have been able to achieve success
3.   therefore, mainstream media objectively reports on those who perform well within the meritocracy, using logical statistics and results as a guide, thereby eliminating racism

Sports are competitive like many facets of our society and victory serves as its own natural ultimate equalizer, but what if the game were rigged? What would be the point in competing then? Nationwide mainstream sports media is dominated by white sportswriters, white editors and white producers. Thus, when it comes to mainstream sports coverage, many nonwhite sports figures must see themselves through the lens of others. Period. But is the media considered rigged?

While most sports news is dominated in America by the four top earning leagues (NFL, MLB, NBA & NHL), when it comes to studying racial patterns, the NBA and NFL are of particular interest given these are the only two that boast a majority of nonwhite players.

Given the absence of diverse voices within mainstream sports media, we must remain sensitive to criticisms levied at black players and whether there is a larger subtext at play behind critiques that appear benign, innocuous or logical on the surface (i.e., worst free agent signings = critique of "worth" literally). For within the larger subtext is the historical context of the Unholy Trinity, or rather the centuries-old, race-related thought patterns that have been inculcated throughout American society. Romantic Racialism, Femininity and Negrophobia all have been institutionalized in varying degrees and the ill effects of these thought patterns are still felt today even though the scaffolding originally used to paint these patterns has been long since removed.

Historically, black labor has been dependent upon if not subordinate to whites. Very rarely have blacks as a collective unit consistently and systematically controlled the means of their own production. Arguably, blacks control their bodies. But the way the sports production machine (or conveyor belt) operates, many relinquish full control in exchange for access to greater power and privilege. But in actuality, despite the alluring appearance, many black males do not possess power in "the game" as statistics routinely show that despite rigorous rookie counseling programs, more than half of all black athletes are penniless within five years of playing their last game.[1] How can this be? The player's mindset has been crafted over time; he is not a producer but merely a high-level consumer. While he acquires much that is expensive, he pays for it at a very high price.

More important is that the nonwhite athlete does not exist in a vacuum. Politics and class play a direct part in how games "any given Sunday" play out. With respect to class, it is incontrovertible that the NFL and NBA (NCAA also) all profit from the exploitation of mostly poor black males.[2] With respect to politics, the larger context of racial relations cannot be ignored. How blacks are valued and produce value are integral parts of a complex equation. A proper understanding will allow one to see that although it appears on the surface that these black players are getting "respect," such recognition is as temporary as it is conditional. The players are seen by the owners as fungible "at will" employees. Next man up!

This context allows us to see the six principal patterns by which virtually any nonwhite athlete will be framed within mainstream media. The Sportotypes observe tensions of *fear & fascination, power & control*:

Sportotypes Corresponding with Unholy Trinity					
Menace to Society	Diva		Model Citizen	Comic Relief	Buck
FEAR			FASCINATION		
	Femininity	Romantic Racialism		Femininity	Romantic Racialism
Sportotypes Corresponding with Rigged Game Goals					
POWER			CONTROL		
Menace to Society	Diva		Model Citizen	Comic Relief	Buck

Nonetheless, in answering the rebuttable presumption that "there is NO racism in American sport," the varied and documented examples from the Sportotypes throughout the manuscript indicate that a problematic pattern is indeed at play. While it is true that many a professional black athlete has earned significant sums of money through the sports/entertainment business — this fact alone does not preclude any critical thinking or analysis about the fundamental relationship dynamic between empowered and endowed whites versus mendicant and marginalized blacks. A holistic analysis and reflection of the Sportotypes brings us to these final few rounds where we must wrestle with the possibility that the rebuttable presumption had no chance of ever truly being considered true.

SAME GAME, DIFFERENT NAME?

Presupposing that the rebuttable presumption is false, this means that racism does in fact exist. But how can this be? No hooded Klansmen burn crosses outside of stadiums and fans of all types embrace their coveted players of all types so long as they aid in the enterprise of winning. It is not that fans are immune, but rather in assessing the mainstream media's role in creating and circulating narratives and images about the sports figures we follow, the media has been instrumental in providing pointers to the American public for the transition towards the new game we all play, Racism 2.0.

Keys to the "New Game" of Racism 2.0	
Racism	Racism 2.0
• overt, obvious & offensive	• subtle, suave & sophisticated
Existing Tensions between Racism & Racism 2.0	
• more obvious vs. less offensive	
• historical basis vs. present oasis	
• similar messaging vs. different methodology	
• linear progress vs. literal progress	

More Obvious vs. Less Offensive

Consider how current, sleek, slow-motion, high definition videos of top NBA players soaring through the air to dunk or rising to make long-distance three-pointers differ markedly from "old school" black and white footage of players dribbling, passing and playing the game that Dr. James Naismith first envisioned (especially when dunking and three-point shooting were not part of the original game).[3] Yet, the concept in both is consistent; while stylistically they differ, both media convey the game of basketball.

It follows that any history book from any American high school will reveal that earlier in this country, the "name of the game" for nonwhites competing for the American Dream was racism. Old racism was overt, obvious and offensive and further, discouraged fair competition for limited resources. Despite numerous tweaks, additions and rule changes, the question remains: "Over time, has the game fundamentally changed? Or do we not play the same game by a different name?"

With respect to the NBA and NFL and their high percentage of black players, tensions over *power & control* of "the product" or scintillating and exciting packaged play by a majority nonwhite labor force remain. The painfully obvious truth is that whites originally enslaved blacks as a captive labor force against their will and with the aid of white-dominated legal, economic, educational and social institutions, denied blacks full dignity, respect and access to the American Dream. During our country's founding it was *more obvious* that whites were dominant and blacks were subjugated and suppressed. Now, players make millions. But owners make billions.

How the "Slavery" Analogy *Might* Work

- poor black males exploited "in the field" once again

- cycle of temporary nonwhite riches in contrast to permanent wealth of white owner

- most dangerous work (e..g, shortest careers 3.5 years)

- highest injury/disability rate

- minimal free time; shrunken sphere of autonomy on/off the "job"

- thorough "inspections" before being picked (drafted) by the highest bidder

- personnel are told to strip down before being picked at draft (auction)

- personnel are put on an elevated social platform & publicly displayed before being selected

- the work product which the player creates is ultimately owned by the owner

Fast-forwarding to today, despite numerous changes, whites are still dominant in ownership and administration of all of the top sports leagues and of the media that covers them. This continued relational dynamic of white dominated *power & control* over under-leveraged black labor has prompted many a black professional athlete over the years[4] to invoke the historical reference of slavery in spite of the fact that today's black athlete provides their labor to the market through a system that is highly stylized and glamorized and therefore *less offensive.* Who wouldn't want to live the fabulous life of a NBA star, right?

Historical Basis vs. Present Oasis

Today, we have the benefit of hindsight and distancing through time to reflect upon racist tactics of the past. The league-wide celebration of Jackie Robinson Day in MLB for example,[5] recognizes that American mainstream sport in fact had a *historical basis* in racism. However, since racism over time has successfully been branded as offensive and undesirable, if and when it does re-appear within contemporary society, corporate actors especially race to isolate such acts within a *present oasis,* so that such events are interpreted as individualistic and not institutional.

For instance, "back in the day," many a professional franchise owner harbored questionable ideas about black labor (e.g., Marge Schott and Georgia Frontiere). Times do change. Yet, not everything changes. Consider former NBA Atlanta Hawks General Manager Danny Ferry's casual comments that came to light through the new technology of social media.[6] Eventually, Ferry personally took the fall and the Hawks franchise moved forward. It is unknown to what degree the franchise continues to operate within the diplomatic, yet dismissive Ferry mindset, even though it is not reported upon.

Similar Messaging vs. Different Methodology

One of the key tensions in making the provocative and possibly offensive "slavery analogy" is the idea that today, professional athletes are "professional," trained and paid handsomely for their services. Today's "professional defense" takes care to distance itself from *similar messaging* from the past that invoked imagery of flagrant exploitation of another (especially when based upon race or "color").

But does flagrant exploitation of mostly under-leveraged and disenfranchised black laborers still take place via a *different methodology?* Add in eye-opening revelations like University of Florida coach Billy Donovan's new $3.7 million-a-year contract and the $18,000 bonus that Ohio State athletic director Gene Smith received for one of the school's wrestlers winning an NCAA title, and it gets harder for some to sympathize with the NCAA's contention that everything it does is for the benefit of athletes who play for the glory of their schools.[7] The methodology is "amateurism" and the "spirit of competition" as a value-added benefit to the true gift of a free education. Yet, mostly elderly white men still personally profit.

Linear Progress vs. Literal Progress

When judging *linear progress* on a time line, we are by definition more advanced today than what we were in 1992, and 1992 was more advanced than 1974, and 1974 was more advanced than 1954, etc. More important than merely ticking off the quantity of years as a definitive measure of progress in and of itself, the quality of progress over time is at issue. Again, the appearance of progress and the presence of progress are two different matters. When the NBA first started, it discriminated against black players and excluded them from participation. Now, it would be considered blasphemous to field a NBA team without black players, although in MLB this is "normal." Consider what former National League MVP and black MLB Pittsburgh Pirates player, Andrew McCutcheon said about youthful fans having access to play the game of baseball: (https://www.yahoo.com/sports/blogs/mlb-big-league-stew/andrew-mccutchen-says-baseball-is-freezing-out-lower-income-kids-025505358.html).

Yet, in looking at the white dominated power ranks of owners, administration and media (e.g., proprietorship, patronage and press), it begs the question of what is the *literal progress* of blacks relative to whites if they are still subjugated to dominant white male *power & control* dynamics off the court or field, despite appearing to dominate on the actual basketball court or football field.

PLAYING WITH PAIN

Not to be a "bad sport," but it is important to recall that there was a time when America was in fact racist (i.e., Era of Enslavement perhaps?). Today is a new day. But how new? There is desperation on both benches of Team White and Team Black. Team White is desperate to move on and seeks to avoid any costly, exhausting or draining overtime periods or sudden death scenarios, while members of Team Black are desperate to have the referees review and replay key fouls from earlier in the game that became momentum shifters and perhaps unfairly influenced the outcome of the game. Will whites ever "grant" blacks the satisfaction of admitting when something really is racist? Do blacks need whites to validate racism?

Similar to race in movies, we periodically receive these reports that tell us how much better the racial landscape is. But what if the "slavery analogy," as distasteful as it sounds or appears, is credible in some shape or form? Even if found incredible, the fact remains that in this country, any institution that requires large scale racial integration will require critical analysis about how much race is a factor in final decision-making and with the final products produced.

Given the sobering statistical data surrounding black life in America and the continuing disparities blacks suffer (e.g., housing, education, life expectancy, etc.) it is prudent to question why nowhere else except in sports/entertainment is there a demand for black professionals (e.g., as opposed to lawyers, doctors). While LeBron's "Decision" may have been a questionable call, at the same time maybe all it was, was a bad public relations move. The over-reaction experienced and witnessed (i.e., burning of jerseys) during the aftermath was perhaps racially flavored — especially if you take the time to read some of these "neutral" posts by anonymous and faceless fans. Similar patterns appear with Woods' adultery and Vick's dogfighting cases. These athletes undoubtedly engaged in inappropriate behavior. Yet, we seldom scrutinize whether they were subject to inappropriate reactions. They are neither the first nor the last to commit these acts.

So what remains painful is the idea that nonwhite, high profile athletes must bear the cost for this additional burden of the *colleague vs. collared* approach; within professional sports whites do not respect black men inasmuch as they protect black men while temporarily able to profit from them or extract a personal benefit:

COLLEAGUE vs. COLLARED APPROACH TO WHITE/NONWHITE RELATIONS
NON-WHITES ARE CONDITIONED TO:
Revere, fear and many cases endear themselves to white men.
WHITES ARE CONDITIONED TO:
Cheer, jeer and in many cases leer at nonwhite (black) men.

Many sensible whites who were "raised the right way," and who "do not see racism," remain puzzled over racist flares that appear in mainstream media on occasion. Exclamations of "Where did this come from?" and "Oh! I didn't know!" typically position whites and their innate exceptionalist optimism to "require proof" of racism, otherwise, a "perfectly reasonable explanation" exists for the action in question. While every vague and unfounded accusation cannot be treated seriously, the default skepticism of racism creates a doubly damaging burden upon the victim to prove the "perfect case." For example, when a black male complains of discrimination in the marketplace when searching for a job, is this too vague a claim? Or does a study sending out resumes with "black sounding names" with worse results than identical resumes with "white sounding names" then move the needle?[8] Does data now make the original complaints any more credible? If so, for who? For even without the study, would the end resultant effect be any less damaging for the black male?

In other words, within the meritocracy driven world of sport, it is similarly difficult to isolate and pinpoint instances of *Racism 2.0*. The Sportotypes will aid and enlist with the enterprise of engaging in further study. For when young mostly white teenagers in high school basketball gyms all across our country chant "Where's your green card?" to Latino players, "Soy sauce" and "Small eyes" to Asian American players, "Slurpees" to Arab American players and "GPA" to black players, perhaps the perfectly reasonable explanation for the action is in fact racism.[9]

When white American "fans of the game" plan ahead, go to a grocery store, purchase tickets to a sporting event, remember to pack their produce, arrive at the stadium and toss bananas out on the baseball field or ice rink at what just happens to be black players, perhaps the perfectly logical explanation is in fact racism.[10]

TIME TO HANG UP THE CLEATS?

In concluding our manuscript's introductory analysis on the relationship between Race & Sports, we conclude with a name forever linked with race, races and racism: *Owens*. The late great Olympian Jesse Owens won four gold medals in Nazi Germany during the Berlin Summer Games of 1936. Upon returning home to the United States, Owens remarked "But what was I supposed to do? I had four gold medals, but you can't eat four gold medals."[11] Owens succinctly referenced the fact that superseding competition on the track did not exempt him from racism in America that remained firmly on track.

Another Owens, former legend of the legendary NFL Philadelphia Eagles, Terrell Owens, commented that racism was a factor in NFL Dallas Cowboys wide receiver Dez Bryant receiving hypercriticism.[12] Owens comments were promptly and roundly dismissed. Yet, is it possible he is correct? After all, he was accurate when determining exactly when to jump for a ball, when to extend his hands to secure a ball, when to accelerate and how fast, how to maneuver past would-be tacklers in real time, so what about the possibility those same skills could be applied accurately towards social matters off the field?

The mere existence of both Owens indicates that evolution, not elimination of racism is what we are presently experiencing, just like with all other facets of "the game." This conversation is in no danger of being "shutout" anytime soon. Debating the elimination of racism in mainstream sport is akin to arguing who's better? "Bird or Magic?"

If we wish to "win" this debate, we may someday break through the way the Boston Red Sox finally broke the Bambino curse...but what if the situation is akin to the Chicago Cubs?[13] What shall we do then?

A
PPENDIX

<u>BOX SCORE</u>

Endnotes, MLA Style

Chapter Zero References, pp. 2-10

1. "Say it ain't so, Joe" relates to an urban legend whereby early twentieth century Chicago White Sox player "Shoeless" Joe Jackson was accused of fixing baseball games and was asked this question by a disheartened young fan in disbelief as Jackson walked out the courtroom after the grand jury entered an indictment. To show how popular this sports phrase is within mainstream pop culture, the Guerilla Opera in Boston created a production entitled "Say It Ain't So, Joe": David Weininger. "'Say It Ain't So, Joe' Based on Palin-Biden Debate on CD." Boston Globe. Web. 24, February, 2012. <https://www.bostonglobe.com/arts/2012/02/24/say-ain-joe-opera-based-palin-biden-debate/pesd3LtLpFF5DyYbcchJ5O/story.html>.

2. Sabermetrics is the intense analysis of theoretical baseball statistics as a predictor of practical game success. The 2011 movie "Moneyball" dealt with this revolutionary approach to data use starred Brad Pitt and Jonah Hill.

3. Sean Highkin. "NBA's New Tracking Stats Give Fans a Window to the Future." USA Today. Web. 1 November, 2013. < http://www.usatoday.com/story/sports/nba/2013/11/01/nba-analytics-sportvu-cameras-stats-chris-paul/3358057/>.

4. "Jim McKay, Olympics and ABC Announcer, Dies at Age 86." ESPN.com News Services. Web. 8 June, 2008. < http://espn.go.com/espn/news/story?id=3430672>.

5. Check out the following links for instances of international racism in sport:
- Italian baseball team in blackface: https://www.youtube.com/watch?v=FjOdMzbt17g
- Unruly Chelsea soccer fans: http://www.msn.com/en-us/sports/soccer/group-of-soccer-fans-prevent-black-man-from-boarding-train/ar-BBhHTNd
- Belgian insults: http://soccernet.espn.go.com/news/story?id=652062&&cc=5901
- European [Golf] Tour Players Awards Dinner: http://www.golfchannel.com/news/joe-posnanski/garcias-fried-chicken-remark-shows-disdain-woods/
- Russia black out: http://news.yahoo.com/russia-bans-black-player-reacting-racism-131414481.html
- Canadian bacon: http://www.cbc.ca/m/news/canada/manitoba/icing-racism-in-hockey-players-speak-out-1.2831319

6. NHL Philadelphia Flyers' winger Wayne Simmonds had a banana tossed at him right before he took a penalty shot in a game against the Detroit Red Wings during an exhibition game played in London, Ontario in 2011. Simmonds upon reflection noted, "When you're black, you kind of expect (racist) things. You learn to deal with it." "Support Flows in for Simmonds after Incident." NHL.com. Web. 23 September, 2011. < https://www.nhl.com/news/support-flows-in-for-simmonds-after-incident/c-589495>.

7. Check out the following links for past instances of American racism in sport (with the exception of the first, all of the other examples take place before the year 2000):

- Venus and Serena Williams and their family have recorded and documented instances of disparaging racial epithets articulated in their honor: <http://www.theroot.com/articles/culture/2014/10/insulting_venus_and_serena_isn_t_anything_new.html>; <http://www.miaminewtimes.com/2010-09-16/news/venus-and-serena-williams-suffer-racism/full/; http://www.vox.com/2015/3/11/8189679/serena-williams-indian-wells racism>.
- In 1999, Atlanta Braves closer John Rocker on New York City: "The biggest thing I don't like about New York are the foreigners. You can walk an entire block in Times Square and not hear anybody speaking English. Asians and Koreans and Vietnamese and Indians and Russians and people and everything up there. How the hell did they get in this country?" <https://web.archive.org/web/20000817193712/http://sportsillustrated.cnn.com/features/cover/news/1999/12/22/rocker/>.
- In 1993, Cincinatti Reds owner Marge Schott referred to black star players Eric Davis and Dave Parker as her "Million dollar n*ggers": < http://reds.enquirer.com/1998/10/102598sabo.html>.
- In 1992, Fuzzy Zoeller in reference to [PGA] Masters tradition of reigning winner Tiger Woods setting the menu for following year: "Tell him not to serve fried chicken next year. Got it? Or collard greens or whatever the hell they serve." < https://www.youtube.com/watch?v=9ufpU3X-t4w>.
- In 1988, NFL football analyst Jimmy the Greek on live television: The black is a better athlete to begin with because he's been bred to be that way, because of his high thighs and big thighs that goes up into his back, and they can jump higher and run faster because of their bigger thighs and he's bred to be the better athlete because this goes back all the way to the Civil War when during the slave trade ... the slave owner would breed his big black to his big woman so that he could have a big black kid." < https://www.youtube.com/watch?v=WzB7IsmOegE>.
- In 1983, Howard Cosell on Monday Night Football about black Washington Redsk*ns receiver Alven Garrett: "That little monkey gets loose, doesn't he?!" < https://www.youtube.com/watch?v=Bhq_eNUYSZ0>.

8. See the Infographic slide show with national data assembled in "Race Equality in America: How Far Have We Come?" The Christian Science Monitor. Web. Last updated 21 August 2014. < http://www.csmonitor.com/Photo-Galleries/Infographics/Race-equality-in-America-How-far-have-we-come>.

9. "With Barack Obama ensconced as the nation's first black president, plenty of voices in the national conversation are trumpeting America as a post-racial society -- that race matter (sic) much less than it used to, that the boundaries of race have been overcome, that racism is no longer a big problem." Lum, Lydia. "The Obama Era: A Post-Racial Society?" Diverse Issues in Higher Education. 25:26 (Feb 5, 2009): 14-16.

Chapter 1 References, pp. 12-22

1. Manifest Destiny is defined as "the right of America to 'conquer, colonize, and Christianize' the continent of North America." Buck, Christopher. Religious Myths and Visions of America: How Minority Faiths Redefined America's World Role. Westport, CT: Praeger Publishers, 2009, p. 8.

2. For integration dates for the major pro sports, see "Integration Milestones in Pro Sports." ESPN. Web. 25 February 2002. < http://espn.go.com/ gen/s/2002/0225/1340314.html>.

3. William C. Rhoden. Forty Million Dollar Slaves: The Rise, Fall, and Redemption of the Black Athlete. New York: Three Rivers Press, 2006.

4. The United States of America has a long, documented and protracted history of Whites exacting control over Black bodies. For a historical narrative on the intersectionality of black male labor/public displays of masculinity, see Howard Zinn. A People's History of the United States: 1492 - Present. New York: HarperCollins Publishers, 2003; James W. Loewen. Lies My Teacher Told Me: Everything Your American History Textbook Got Wrong. New York: Touchstone, 2007; Michelle Alexander. The New Jim Crow: Mass Incarceration in the Age of Colorblindness. New York: The New Press, 2012.

5. Not only are the darts typically dull, but the balloons are also underinflated. "Learn the Tricks to Be a Winner at State Fair Midway." WFAA Staff. Web. 16 October, 2009. < http://legacy.wfaa.com/story/news/local/2014/08/06/13437246/>.

6. Throw with vigor; bottom pins can be as heavy as ten pounds apiece! Sid Kirchheimer. "7 Rigged Carnival Games." AARP. Web. 17 July, 2012. < http://www. aarp.org/money/scams-fraud/info-07-2012/rigged-carnival-games.html>.

7. See Forrest Wickman. "How Do You Win the Claw Game?" Slate.com. Web. 7 February, 2012. < http://www.slate.com/articles/news_and_politics/explainer/2012/02/ australian_boy_noah_jeffrey_climbs_inside_of_a_carnival_claw_game_how_do_ you_win_those_things_anyway_.html>.

8. See endnote #8 from Chapter Zero.

9. Joe Rodgers. "Patriots 'Bracing' for Tom Brady to Lose Deflategate Appeal, Report Says." SportingNews.com. Web. 13 March, 2016. < http://www.sportingnews.com/ nfl-news/4698257-patriots-tom-brady-lose-deflategate-latest-appeal-serve-4-game- suspension>.

10. Mink, Gwendolyn; Alice O'Connor. Poverty in the United States: An Encyclopedia of History, Politics, and Policy, Volume 1. Santa Barbara, CA: ABC-CLIO, Inc., 2004.

11. See Chapter Four, "Uncle Tom and the Anglo-Saxons: Romantic Racialism in the North." Fredrickson, George. The Black Image in the White Mind: The Debate on Afro-American Character and Destiny, 1817-1914. New York: Harper & Row, 1971.

12. Id., p. 114.

13. "Uncle Tom's Cabin remains the world's second most translated book, after the Bible." Hollis Robbins. "Uncle Tom's Cabin and the Matter of Influence." The Gilder Lehrman Institute of American History. Web. N.d. < https://www.gilderlehrman.org/ history-by-era/literature-and-language-arts/essays/uncle-tom's-cabin-and-matter- influence>.

14. The Black Image in the White Mind, Chapter Nine, "Negro as Beast: Southern Negrophobia at the Turn of the Century."

15. "Lynching in America: Confronting the Legacy of Racial Terror," Equal Justice Initiative. Equal Justice Initiative, 2015. Web. 12 December, 2015. < http://www.eji.org/files/EJI%20Lynching%20in%20America%20SUMMARY.pdf>.

Also, see by Cynthia Skove Nevels, Lynching to Belong: Claiming Whiteness through Racial Violence. Centennial Series of the Association of Former Students, Texas A&M University, 2007. With case studies of lynchings fueled by early Irish and Italian immigrants, the premise offered is that the more racist outside immigration groups were, the more they proved their "Americanness" for mainstream inclusion.

16. Jeffrey B. Perry, ed. A Hubert Harrison Reader. Middletown, CT: Wesleyan University Press, 2001, p. 54.

17. "The Horatio Alger myth has become emblematic of the American Dream." Art Silverblatt, Jane Ferry, Barbara Finan. Approaches to Media Literacy: A Handbook. New York: Routledge, 2009, p. 205.

18. For instance, the Brookins Institute wondered hypothetically "What would Martin Luther King Jr. think of America in 2015 if he'd lived to see his eighty-sixth birthday?" concluding that "King would be disturbed by the stubborn race gaps that remain, especially in opportunity, tarnishing the idea of the American Dream. In terms of opportunity, there are still two Americas, divided by race." The study noted that· 1) half of black Americans born poor stay poor, 2) most black middle class kids are downwardly mobile, 3) black wealth barely exists, 4) most black families headed by single parent and 5) black students attend worse schools. Richard V. Reeves and Edward Rodrigue. "Five Bleak Facts on Black Opportunity." Brookings. Web. 15 January 2015.

19. The University of Chicago conducted a study entitled "Are Emily and Brendan More Employable than Lakisha and Jamal?" with the finding that white-sounding names are 50% more likely to get called back for an initial interview than identical applicants with black sounding names. Erza Klein. "Racism Isn't Over. But Policymakers from both Parties Like to Pretend It Is." The Washington Post. Web. 1 December 2013. < https://www.washingtonpost.com/news/wonk/wp/2013/12/01/racism-isnt-over-but-policymakers-from-both-parties-like-to-pretend-it-is/>.

To learn how it is easier for a white convict to obtain a call back for an interview compared to a black applicant with no criminal record, also see Paul Von Zielbauer. "Race a Factor in Job Offers for Ex-Convicts." The New York Times. Web. 17 June 2005. < http://www.nytimes.com/2005/06/17/nyregion/race-a-factor-in-job-offers-for-exconvicts.html>.

Chapter 2 References, pp. 24-34

1. Daniel Kaplan. "NFL Projecting Revenue Increase of $1B over 2014." Street & Smith's Sports Business Journal. Web. 9 March 2015. < http://www.sportsbusinessdaily. com/Journal/Issues/2015/03/09/Leagues-and-Governing-Bodies/NFL-revenue.aspx>.

2. "Draft Day" is a 2014 movie starring Academy Award winner Kevin Costner and Jennifer Garner. < http://www.draftdaythemovie.com>.

3. See the following links: NBA: http://www.usatoday.com/story/sports/ nba/2013/06/25/nba-racial-and-gender-report-richard-lapchick/2456481/; NFL: https://www.aei.org/publication/overall-the-nfl-gets-a-letter-grade-of-a-for-race-but-for-kickers-and-punters-wouldnt-the-nfl-get-an-f/ ; MLB: http://m.mlb.com/news/ article/44425610/study-decline-in-number-of-african-american-players-in-mlb-overstated ; NHL: http://www.npr.org/sections/codeswitch/2015/02/26/389284068/ as-first-black-american-nhl-player-enforcer-was-defenseless-vs-racism.

4. The black population as of 2014 is 13.2%. "QuickFacts." United States Census Bureau. Web. N.d. < http://www.census.gov/quickfacts/>.

5. Henry Abbott. "LeBron James' Decision: the Transcript." ESPN. Web. 9 July 2010. < http://espn.go.com/blog/truehoop/post/_/id/17853/lebron-james-decision-the-transcript>.

6. See the following links: http://fivethirtyeight.com/features/the-2128-native-american-mascots-people-arent-talking-about/; http:// indiancountrytodaymedianetwork.com/2014/09/21/report-says-more-2000-native-american-mascots-are-not-contested-15698; http://news.yahoo.com/california-school-retires-divisive-arab-mascot-005218146.html.

For continued public debate on the topic of Native American mascot utility, see the following link: <https://www.yahoo.com/sports/news/bomani-jones-makes-statement-indians-085500948.html> where ESPN personality (and black male) Bomani Jones made a counter-statement by wearing a t-shirt on television featuring the lettering "Caucasians" stylized like the word "Indians" in the MLB Cleveland Indians' logo, complete with a blond-haired smiling face and a dollar sign sticking out the back of his head (as opposed to a feather).

7. "2015 Major League Baseball Racial and Gender Report Card." Sports Business News. Web. 15 April 2015. < http://www.sportsbusinessnews.com/node/26907>.

8. Of the four nonwhite owners, half were American "minorities" born and raised in America whereas for the other 118 owners, most are American white males who in pursuit of the Horatio Alger myth, were somehow able to "work their way up."

9. However, the Rooney Rule is not perfect. See Jared Dubin. "The Rooney Rule Appears to Mask a Larger Racial Problem in Coaching. CBSSports.com. Web. 12 January 2016. < http://www.cbssports.com/nfl/eye-on-football/25447163/the-rooney-rule-appears-to-be-masking-a-larger-racial-problem-in-coaching>.

10. Fewer than 9% of top coaches are black even though more than half of all NCAA football players are black. Marc Tracy. "Opportunity Seldom Knocks for Black Football Coaches." The New York Times. Web. 14 December, 2015. < http://www. nytimes.com/2015/12/15/sports/ncaafootball/black-college-football-coaches-see-few-opportunities.html>.

11. The reader must be careful to distinguish attendance at the stadium venue from actual viewership at home, restaurant, etc. Remarkably, accurate and reliable statistical data on this topic was far and few between. The most recent media article with some statistical analysis across the board (and the source for the chart on page 29) was from 1989: NBA 1989 http://articles.philly.com/1989-12-05/sports/26159992_1_blacks-sports-on-television-today-stadium-or-arena. Perhaps the reader can conduct a "bit of research" as well and discover for themselves or hard or easy it is to find a definitive answer to this question. The reader should also consider, why is concrete data for this question so elusive and hard to find?

Scarborough Sports Marketing, based in New York, puts African American turnout at MLB games at 8% of total attendance...One of the few teams that does track attendance of minority fans, the Chicago White Sox, says a mere 4.5% of fans coming through the turnstiles are black -- in a city with an African American population of 37%. See http://www.bloomberg.com/bw/stories/2006-10-01/the-racial-gap-in the-grandstands; http://m.sportsbusinessdaily.com/Daily/Issues/2012/04/16/Leagues-and-Governing-Bodies/MLB.aspx 9% attendance black MLB

NHL attendance records are virtually nonexistent https://books.google.com/bo oks?id=XppFAAAAQBAJ&pg=PA409&dq=blacks+attendance+professional+sp orting+events&hl=en&sa=X&ved=0ahUKEwjOrqORyKrLAhVFymMKHe12A-YQ6AEIIjAB#v=onepage&q=blacks%20attendance%20professional%20sporting%20 events&f=false

12. See Rob Neyer. "Seven Things You Can't Say on (Baseball) Television." SBNation. com. Web. 8 May, 2013. < http://www.sbnation.com/2013/5/8/4312552/dirty-words-baseball-television-george-carlin>. For bonus: https://baseballrevival.wordpress. com/2013/08/02/the-business-mans-special-and-the-art-of-baseball-hooky/.

13. The "Fortune 500" is a list of the top 500 performing American companies primarily within the private sector. As of 2015, "This year's Fortune 500 marks the 61st running of the list. In total, the Fortune 500 companies account for $12.5 trillion in revenues, $945 billion in profits, $17 trillion in market value and employ 26.8 million people worldwide." "Fortune 500." Fortune. Web. 2015. <http://fortune.com/ fortune500/>.

14. National Public Radio reports that Super Bowl XLIX of 2015 was the most watched show in the entire history of the invention called the television. Eyder Peralta. "Super Bowl XLIX Was Most Watched Show in TV History." NPR. 2 February 2015. Web. < http://www.npr.org/sections/thetwo-way/2015/02/02/383352809/super-bowl-xlix-was-most-watched-show-in-tv-history>.

15. See "The Status of Women in the U.S. Media 2014." Women's Media Center. Web. 2014. < http://wmc.3cdn.net/6dd3de8ca65852dbd4_fjm6yck9o.pdf>. The figures for "White" and black include women; for example the Entire Staff was found 73.7% white male in 2012 and 12.3% white female for a total of 86%. In 2012 the total of 6.4% black men and 1.2% black women made for a total of 7.6%.

16. Carefully compare the language employed in these two articles: Josh Dubow. "Derek Carr Calls Debut Start a Learning Experience." Yahoo! Sports. Web. 10 September 2014. < http://sports.yahoo.com/news/derek-carr-calls-debut-start-232427077--nfl.html> versus Frank Schwab. "Perfect Marcus Mariota Outplays Inept Jameis Winston in Their Debuts." Yahoo! Sports. Web. 13 September, 2015. < http://sports.yahoo.com/blogs/nfl-shutdown-corner/perfect-marcus-mariota-outplays-inept-jameis-winston-in-their-debuts-231151931.html>.

17. See the Wall Street Journal's assessment of Jameis Winston and his baggage: http://www.wsj.com/video/jameis-winston-baggage-vs-endorsement-cash/DB8FF52F-3595-4D92-AC24-BEDCE671230D.html.

18. Otherwise known as "cherrypicking." In basketball especially, it is an advantage when a defender does not cross the midcourt line while on defense and essentially "pitches a tent" underneath their own basket, waiting for a long-distance pass from one of the other four defenders who did in fact cross half-court to complete a fast-break opportunity without having truly "earned" the basket.

19. For more information about Venus Hottentot, or Sara Baartman, see: http://www.nytimes.com/2007/01/14/books/review/Elkins.t.html; for Ota Benga, see: https://www.nyu.edu/about/news-publications/nyu-stories/pamela-newkirk-on-ota-benga-at-the-bronx-zoo.html; for background on how Intelligence Quotient tests were used to justify prejudicial conditions and structural inequalities against blacks in school, see: http://www.newsweek.com/iq-189502. To learn of the financial and physical exploitation of Henrietta Lacks, see: http://www.smithsonianmag.com/science-nature/henrietta-lacks-immortal-cells-6421299/?no-ist.

20. As evidenced by this source citation, Tiger Woods' "incident" is beyond just a "sports story" with respect to its sensational mainstream appeal: http://www.intouchweekly.com/posts/tiger-woods-elin-nordegren-cheating-79517.

Chapter 3 References, pp. 36-46

1. Kevin Baker. "NFL: National Felons League." The Wall Street Journal. Web. 4 February 2000. < http://www.wsj.com/articles/SB94962022666901974>.

2. "Dwight Howard License Suspended." ESPN.com News Services. Web. 16 September 2014. < http://espn.go.com/nba/story/_/id/11540366/dwight-howard-florida-driver-license-suspended-outstanding-red-light-ticket>.

3. According to (now) sportsradio talk show host and first time winner of the "Jim Rome Smack Off," JT the Brick informs that Clones or callers phoning in to the Jim Rome show endure wait times of "longer than an hour." In fact, JT the Brick made his infamous winning phone call from his office desk. John "JT the Brick" Tournour and Alan Eisenstock. The Handoff: A Memoir of Two Guys, Sports, and Friendship. New York: Center Street, 2013.

4. See endnote #14, Chapter 2.

5. See the discussion about the "disease" "discovered" by Dr. Samuel Cartwright entitled drapetomia. Fredrickson, George. The Black Image in the White Mind: The Debate on Afro-American Character and Destiny, 1817-1914. New York: Harper & Row, 1971, p.57.

6. See "Slavery by another Name." PBS. Web. N.d. < http://www.pbs.org/tpt/slavery-by-another-name/themes/convict-leasing/>.

7. "By 1925 total Ku Klux Klan membership was about 4 million." Lisa Klobuchar. 1963 Birmingham Church Bombing: The Ku Klux Klan's History of Terror. Mankato, MN: Compass Point Books, 2009. "A group that reached a peak membership of five thousand members, the party not only influenced radicals from every ethnic community in the United States, it inspired marginalized and oppressed people worldwide who created Black Panther Parties." Jeffrey O.G. Ogbar. Black Power: Radical Politics and African American Identity. Baltimore, MD: The Johns Hopkins University Press, 2005, p. 189.

8. Greater mandatory minimum sentences dictated that federal judges impose harsher penalties for crack cocaine offenses in contrast to powder cocaine offenses at a ratio of 100:1. Most crack cocaine offenders were black; most power cocaine offenders were white. For more information about the 100:1 crack cocaine to powder cocaine sentencing ratio, see "Planet Rock: the Story of Hip Hop and the Crack Generation" narrated by Ice-T <https://www.youtube.com/watch?v=BWKo8CLL3ks>.

9. See Katharine Q. Seelye. "In Heroin Crisis, White Families Seek Gentler War on Drugs." The New York Times. Web. 30 October, 2015. < http://www.nytimes.com/2015/10/31/us/heroin-war-on-drugs-parents.html>.

10. Analysis conducted by the U.S. Sentencing Commission showed that black males are dealt with more harshly, receiving prison sentences nearly 20% longer than white men for similar crimes. Joe Palazzolo. "Racial Gap in Men's Sentencing." The Wall Street Journal. Web. 14 February 2013. <http://www.wsj.com/articles/SB10001424127887324443200457830446378985800 2>.

11. Tiger Woods once referred to himself as "Cablinasian" as it properly encompassed his Caucasian, Indian, Asian and Black ancestry. However, Mr. Woods does not necessarily have the "final" say in his own identity. Much of the rhetoric and racial incidents involving Mr. Woods has been over his external "black" appearance. Oliver Brown. "Why Tiger Woods Refused to Play the Race Card against His Former Caddie Steve Williams." The Telegraph. Web. 9 November, 2011. < http://www.telegraph.co.uk/sport/golf/tigerwoods/8879865/Why-Tiger-Woods-refused-to-play-the-race-card-against-his-former-caddie.html>.

12. Valerie Strauss. "19 States Still Allow Corporal Punishment in School." The Washington Post. Web. 18 September, 2014. <https://www.washingtonpost.com/news/answer-sheet/wp/2014/09/18/19-states-still-allow-corporal-punishment-in-school/>.

13. "Law & Order: SVU": https://tv.yahoo.com/blogs/tv-news/chad-coleman-law--order--svu-ray-rice-walking-dead-224252653.html; President Obama on Ray Rice scandal: "Hitting a woman" is not what "a real man does," <http://chicago.suntimes.com/politics/obama-on-ray-rice-hitting-a-woman-not-what-a-real-man-does/>.

14. See "Estimated 7,000 Fans Trade in Ray Rice Jerseys." USA Today. Web. 20 September, 2014. <http://www.usatoday.com/story/sports/nfl/2014/09/20/estimated-7-000-fans-trade-in-ray-rice-jerseys/15961241/>.

15. Jeremy Fowler. "Protesters speak out against Steelers' signing of Michael Vick." ESPN. Web. 26 August, 2015. <http://espn.go.com/nfl/story/_/id/13519067/protesters-speak-pittsburgh-steelers-signing-michael-vick>.

16. Perfect game Chicago White Sox pitcher Mark Buehrle loves dogs so much, he has gone on record defending his statement that he watches Michael Vick play football in hopes of seeing him get hurt as repayment for Vick's role within the dogfighting ring: http://profootballtalk.nbcsports.com/2011/02/17/mark-buehrle-on-hoping-michael-vick-gets-hurt-i-said-it-i-meant-it/. It is unknown whether Buehrle is a strong animal advocate or just dogs in particular. If the former, it would be interesting to get Buehrle's take on cock fighting. FYI, cock fighting is a billion dollar-a-year industry still legal in three states: http://abcnews.go.com/WNT/story?id=131142&page=1.

17. For another example of the mainstream public's sensitivity over black males and white females, see this link featuring Owens and Desperate Housewives star Nicollette Sheridan in a 2004 "sexy" opening of Monday Night Football: https://www.youtube. com/watch?v=FcED1iRbj_c. While Terrell Owens was approached by others at ABC Sports who conceptualized the idea, performed revisions, filmed it, proofed it, edited it, and decided to broadcast it, it is nonetheless he who takes the heat and criticism for the sketch's "failure." ABC Sports, in response to the backlash and controversy, later deemed the bit "inappropriate" and apologized (http://usatoday30.usatoday. com/sports/football/nfl/2004-11-16-mnf-intro-apology_x.htm). The reaction by the mostly white dominated media and proactive fan base raises the question of whether the skit itself was misogynistic, or decidedly so when the "beneficiary" was a black male. In other words, at the time, Desperate Housewives was a top-rated show that featured white males and white women engaging in sordid and desperate affairs. This was top-ranked entertainment. But the sight of a white blond woman dropping her towel and jumping in a black male's arms crossed the line of appropriateness, meaning, mainstream America was not that desperate for interracial risque behavior. Such behavior currently should apparently be reserved for whites only.

18. Three additional examples of professional (black) athletes being regarded as presumed criminals or threats include: 1) NFL Seattle Seahawks player Cam Chancellor was looking to PURCHASE a gymnasium and instead had occupants dial 911 when he peered in the window after no one answered the door: http://www.seattletimes.com/sports/seahawks/seahawks-kam-chancellor-on-911-incident-just-crazy-how-you-have-to-go-through-that-in-2016/; 2) NBA Milwaukee Bucks center John Henson was looking to purchase an expensive Rolex watch downtown at a jewelry store only to have employees inside "pretend" they were closed as they also dialed 911: http://abcnews.go.com/Sports/pretending-closed-911-calls-released-alleged-racial-prejudice/story?id=34803797; 3) Minnesota State Representative Pat Garofalo tweeted out on social media that most NBA teams could fold and "nobody would notice a difference w/possible exception of increase in streetcrime": http://www.wkow.com/story/24932311/2014/03/10/lawmaker-catching-heat-for-nba-tweet often-felsty.

In all three of the preceding examples, direct criminal associations were made with black professional sports players. In fact, professional sports status did little to protect the victims in these cases from being nonetheless humiliated PUBLICLY. In the first two cases, the bitter irony is that the black male actually has the capital and financial means to purchase what the white (women) working inside likely could not (provided they are salaried employees at these establishments). The blanket aspersion by the LAWMAKER provides a telling clue that he sees himself perhaps "playing defense" on behalf of Team White which is now relentlessly assaulted by scary black males (Negrophobia anyone?). It is difficult to imagine Garofalo making similar comments about the MLB or NHL only because similar comments are not generally made about the MLB and NHL.

19. Maureen Dowd. "Miami's Hoops Cartel." The New York Times. Web. 10 July 2010. <http://www.nytimes.com/2010/07/11/opinion/11dowd.html>.

20. Anwar S. Richardson. "Trent Richardson Learned about Trade from Browns to Colts on the Radio." Yahoo! Sports. Web. 19 September, 2013. <http://sports.yahoo.com/blogs/nfl-shutdown-corner/trent-richardson-learned-trade-browns-colts-radio-125110397--nfl.html>.

See also: Williams Scott Davis. "Steve Smith Says He Found Out He Was Cut On The Radio, Rips The Panthers." Yahoo! Sports. Web. 1 October 2014. http://sports.yahoo.com/news/steve-smith-says-found-cut-204800830.html

Chapter 4 References, pp. 48-58

1. Cork Gaines. "Michael Sam's NFL Future Doesn't Look Good." Business Insider. Web. 2 September, 2014. <http://www.businessinsider.com/michael-sams-nfl-future-2014-9>.

2. Ed Hinton. "Drivers May Not be Athletes, but What They Do is No Game." ESPN. 23 August, 2008. Web. <http://espn.go.com/racing/nascar/cup/columns/story?id=3539848&columnist=hinton_ed>.

3. Psychological professionals are divided; some see "aggressive" sports such as football as not releasing anger and tension, but rather ironically increasing one's capacity to wield anger and tension. Our analysis differs. There is a distinct socio-econo-political impetus that provides Catharsis for those who obtain instant gratification and feedback about their place, value and power within society relative to others who compete in "aggressive" sports such as football and basketball. Historical data has yet to show otherwise.

4. See endnote #5, Chapter 3.

5. With Black Codes cropping up in the aftermath of the Civil War, black life itself was literally criminalized. See "Black Codes and Pig Laws." PBS. Web. N.d. <http://www. pbs.org/tpt/slavery-by-another-name/themes/black-codes/>.

6. Impudence was "one of the greatest crimes of which a slave can be guilty. Does he ever venture to suggest a different mode of doing things from that pointed out by his master? He is indeed presumptuous, and getting above himself." Jennifer Ritterhouse. Growing Up Jim Crow: How Black and White Southern Children Learned Race. Chapel Hill, NC: University of North Carolina Press, 2006, p. 34.

7. "The House always wins" is a phrase reminiscent of the poker/gambling gaming industry that essentially states that no matter how far in front one may appear to be with their winnings, eventually the law of averages bears out that the individual will lose more money than they win the longer they stay to gamble. Here, the phrase refers to the fact that in the "game of wits" between impudent black male athletes and a castigating white male press, often black males will gamble and have public manuevers and displays of bravado pay off, but only temporarily. Very few black male "rebels" within the sports world survive with their rebellious character in tact. From Terrell Owens (https://www.youtube.com/watch?v=X1KsBdkZDjA) to Ricky Watters ("For who, for what?") to Mike Tyson (https://www.youtube.com/watch?v=KG-xC8Mu6SM), White males ultimately hold the power of the pen. The House always wins.

Chapter 5 References, pp. 60-70

1. Julius W. Erving with Karl Taro Greenfeld. Dr. J: the Autobiography. New York: HarperCollins, 2013, p.402.

2. In an editorial, the Pultizer Prize-winning journalist and author of "Friday Night Lights" observed: "When I wrote the book Friday Night Lights about high-school football in Texas, I saw the racial stereotypes of some whites up close—their firm belief that white athletes admirably succeeded because of hustle and hard work and brains, and black athletes succeeded solely on the basis of pure athletic skill. In other words, white athletes virtuously worked their tails off whereas black athletes simply coasted because they can." See Buzz Bissinger. "Here's the Real Reason the NBA is Losing Fans." Business Insider. Web. 18 February 2011. <http://www.businessinsider.com/heres-the-real-reason-the-nba-is-losing-fans-2011-2>.

3. John Carvalho. "Sports Media is Still Racist against Black Athletes." Vice Sports. Web. 3 October, 2014. < https://sports.vice.com/en_us/article/sports-media-is-still-racist-against-black-athletes>. Conduct your own independent investigation to discover: "Is the mainstream sports establishment as critical of white draft picks within MLB and NHL as it is of black draft picks within the NBA and NFL?" The entire structural dynamics and the pressure to perform for immediate financial gain is different within NBA/NFL than it is in MLB/NHL where players have "more time" to develop under "farm systems," thereby encouraging a supportive pressure environment where the hope is that an investment up front will pay off in the end. In contrast equally as young if not younger black players, often facing insurmountable odds along with the requisite burdens of the Unholy Trinity, are under more scrutiny and suppressive pressure to immediately pay off up front on a possible further investment on the back end. Additionally, MLB fantasy leagues operate off a broader, longer time scale and NHL fantasy leagues are not nearly as popular as NFL fantasy leagues whereby mostly white male "fans" become invested and therefore quite attentive and critical about individual black male performance in exchange for points. Meanwhile, NHL players literally skate by on a nightly basis with their ability to make mistakes intact. Search and see whether white NFL players receive similar or greater scrutiny and criticism for their expected performance.

Consider the rhetoric supplied by this white male "fantasy league expert" about a black NFL player: "Still a relatively youthful 31-years-old, most would believe he's destined to pad those stats over the next few seasons. However, his impatient fantasy owners would vehemently disagree, yours truly included." The author goes on to flatly state that this player is "expendable in 12-team leagues." Who is this player? Why none other than Hall of Fame "lock," Larry Fitzgerald. Strong words from a casual fan who unlikely receives parallel public scrutiny of his personal performance within a public purview. See Brad Evans. "Why It's Time to Drop a Longtime Fantasy Standout." Yahoo! Sports. Web. 20 October, 2014. <http://sports.yahoo.com/blogs/yahoo-sports-fantasy-minute/why-it-s-time-to-drop-a-long-time-fantasy-standout-220009158.html>.

4. Blacks did not truly become lazy until they stopped working for free. In other words, stereotypical images of the slothful, incompetent non-working negro were not created and popularized until after blacks were no longer formally enslaved within society. For an historical example, be sure to look at this poster attacking Radical Republicans and their support for Reconstruction in the aftermath of the Civil War in the late 19th century. Only after the Era of Enslavement ended, is the black male depicted as not working while, "The white man must work to keep his children and pay his taxes." What is painfully ironic about this poster is that it was created in 1866, merely one year after enslavement ended which meant that the very definition of a worker was one with black identity, as they had no other lot in life except to work from "can't see" in the morning until "can't see" at night, under the divine principles of Manifest Destiny, of course. See Library of Congress. "The Freedman's Bureau! An agency to keep the Negro in idleness at the expense of the white man. Twice vetoed by the President, and made a lawy by Congress. Support Congress & you support the Negro Sustain the President & you protect the white man." Web. N.d. < http://www. loc.gov/pictures/item/2008661698/>.

Little known is how hard black athletes work off the court and field to combat this perception: Oseguera, L. (2010). Success despite the image: How African American male student-athletes endure their academic journey amidst negative characterizations. Journal for the Study of Sports and Athletes in Education, 4 (3), 297-324.

5. Ben Cohen. "How Brad Stevens Won Boston Without Winning." The Wall Street Journal. Web. 24 February 2016. <http://www.wsj.com/articles/how-brad-stevens-won-boston-without-winning-1456354628>.

6. Pablo S. Torre. "How (and Why) Athletes Go Broke." Sports Illustrated. Web. 23 March, 2009. <http://www.si.com/vault/2009/03/23/105789480/how-and-why-athletes-go-broke>. For a visual treatise on this topic, see "Broke," a 30 for 30 ESPN Film by Billy Corben: https://www.youtube.com/watch?v=gt3HnpJzKAw. Additional links that drive home this painful point are: <https://www.yahoo.com/finance/news/former-nba-player-working-mcdonalds-163907853.html> or <http://sports.yahoo.com/news/getting-shot-at-nfl-could-mean-taking-out-a-loan-064043953.html>.

7. For the purposes of your own independent investigation, consider the nationwide and leaguewide support of the "ice bucket" challenge in support of ALS research (commonly known as Lou Gherig's disease -- Amyotrophic Lateral Sclerosis is colloquially named after a sports figure, a famous New York Yankees baseball player): <http://www.nfl.com/videos/new-york-jets/0ap3000000377538/Jets-take-part-in-Ice-Bucket-Challenge> compared to the isolation experienced by Maurice Jones Drew when he brought attention to the shooting of an unarmed black male teenager named Michael Brown < http://www.csnbayarea.com/raiders/jones-drew-shows-solidarity-hands-dont-shoot>. Said Drew: "My goal is always to create awareness. That's it," Jones Drew said Tuesday. "If I could, I would've tried to be more vocal. But, with my job and what we have to do, it takes away from things you want to do. But, in that moment, I made a stance and I stick with it."

For further study, consider the actions by some black NBA players and the reactions by white fans to players wearing "hoodies" or hooded sweatshirts in honor of the shooting death of another unarmed black male teenager named Trayvon Martin, or of some NBA players wearing black t-shirts with the words "I can't breathe" in white lettering in honor of the choking death literally at the hands of New York City police officers of another unarmed black male named Eric Garner.

Additional links to investigate include: <http://sports.yahoo.com/blogs/nfl-shutdown-corner/washington-redskins-show-support-for-ferguson-in preseason-game-130746001.html>, <http://sports.yahoo.com/blogs/nfl-shutdown-corner/arian-foster-wears-t-shirt-in-support-of-ferguson--mike-brown-during-warmups-140907415.html>; <https://www.yahoo.com/sports/blogs/nfl-shutdown-corner/andrew-hawkins-wears-protest-t-shirt--cleveland-police-aren-t-pleased-004036700.html>; <http://www.salon.com/2014/12/02/bill_oreilly_st_louis_rams_who_protested_arent_smart_enough_to_know_what_theyre_doing/>; <http://sports.yahoo.com/blogs/ncaaf-dr-saturday/ou-coach-bob-stoops-unhappy-with-cb-zack-sanchez-and-message-on-his-headband-203614384.html>.

Compare: <http://www.cbssports.com/nfl/eye-on-football/25165546/did-tom-brady-skip-visit-with-obama-because-hes-mad-at-the-white-house>.

8. Randy Roughton. "Black Airmen Turn Racism, Bigotry into Opportunity." U.S.Air Force. Web. 4 February, 2014. < http://www.af.mil/News/ArticleDisplay/tabid/223/Article/473251/black-airmen-turn-racism-bigotry-into-opportunity.aspx>.

9. The literature on black quarterbacks is quite extensive, from star black college quarterbacks being "converted" (http://www.nfl.com/videos/nfl-combine/0ap2000000144830/Denard-Robinson-on-converting-positions) to being mercilessly criticized publicly (http://sports.yahoo.com/blogs/ncaaf-dr-saturday/florida-state-outlasts-florida-24-19-as-gators-can-t-capitalize-on-seminoles--mistakes-005834943.html) to being ruthlessly analyzed despite apparent indicators of "success" (http://sports.yahoo.com/blogs/ncaaf-dr-saturday/mel-kiper-says-auburn-s-nick-marshall-could-be-4th-or-5th-round-pick-as-a-db-191158331.html) to being cut down to size by children (http://sports.yahoo.com/blogs/nfl-shutdown-corner/young-nfl-fan-takes-cam-newton-to-task-in-elementary-school-newspaper-185703918.html) to being pitied for requiring "training wheels" while learning the offense (http://www.washingtontimes.com/news/2012/aug/25/daly-redskins-keep-training-wheels-rg3-preseason/) to being cajoled for having "fake smiles" (http://profootballtalk.nbcsports.com/2012/06/01/cam-newton-still-wonders-which-sources-said-he-has-a-fake-smile/).

Compare: <http://www.businessinsider.com/carson-wentz-pro-day-throw-2016-3> "[North Dakota State QB] Carson Wentz has seemingly come out of nowhere to have a good shot at being one of the top two picks in the upcoming draft."

Further compare critiques of two different quarterbacks (of two different races) by the same NFL head football coach for the same NFL team (Jay Gruden of the Washington Redsk*ns): Gruden on Robert Griffin III: http://profootballtalk.nbcsports.com/2014/11/23/griffin-could-be-benched-today/?ocid=Yahoo&partner=ya5nbcs; http://sports.yahoo.com/blogs/nfl-shutdown-corner/jay-gruden-has-strong-words-for-robert-griffin-iii-224231305.html versus Gruden on Kirk Cousins: http://national.suntimes.com/national-sports/7/72/1957552/jay-gruden-blames-wind-kirk-cousins-terrible-game/; https://www.washingtonpost.com/sports/redskins/amid-criticism-gruden-has-all-the-confidence-in-the-world-in-cousins/2015/10/19/de144798-76b6-11e5-b9c1-f03c48c96ac2_story.html.

White coaches' harsh criticisms of black players is not limited to the NFL: http://probasketballtalk.nbcsports.com/2014/11/27/hornets-coach-steve-clifford-lance-stephenson-not-a-star/?ocid=Yahoo&partner=ya5nbcs.

10. Deron Snyder. "Black Quarterbacks' Intelligence Still Scrutinized?" The Root. Web. 20 May, 2011. < http://www.theroot.com/articles/culture/2011/05/donovan_mcnabb_wristband_report_intelligence_of_black_quarterbacks_still_debated.html>.

11. "The PGA Tour handed out $101 million in prize money in 1996 (Tiger's last year as an amateur) and $292 million in 2008 (the last year of the Tiger Woods era)." Tony Manfred. "The Tiger Woods Era Made Pro Golfers More Money Than They Could Have Dreamed Of." Business Insider. Web. 2 December 2014. <http://www.businessinsider.com/tiger-woods-era-doubled-pga-tour-prize-money-2014-12>.

12. See Mike Florio. "A Different Kaepernick Met the Media on Wednesday." NBC Sports' Pro Football Talk. Web. 11 December, 2014. <http://profootballtalk.nbcsports. com/2014/12/11/a-different-kaepernick-meets-the-media-on-wednesday/>.

Compare the constant critiques of black males refusing to "comply" with media requests (a la NFL's Seattle Seattle Seahawks Marshawn Lynch) with established, older white respected males within sports circles. White male-dominated media desires access to these men of respect and thus the white male subjects are able to leverage greater power relationships with the media. As an example, consider the stance taken by successful NCAA University of Alabama head football coach, Nick Saban and his refusal to comment on circumstances leading to the suspension of the player Clinton Ha Ha Dix: "'I want to be consistent," he said. "When guys get suspended, I never, ever say what it's for. So I'm not going there. So don't ask me. It's the way it always happens. Every guy. If they do right, they wouldn't be getting suspended. I don't know for how long this will be, so don't ask me that either.'" ESPN.com, "Ha Ha Clinton-Dix Violates Team Rules." Web. 3 October, 2013. < http://espn.go.com/college-football/ story/_/id/9761124/ha-ha-clinton-dix-alabama-crimson-tide-suspended-indefinitely-violation-team-rules>.

13. Mike Triplett. "Saints' Sean Payton misses practice to escort daughter to college." ESPN.com. 26 August, 2015. Web. http://espn.go.com/blog/new-orleans-saints/ post/_/id/17306/saints-sean-payton-misses-practice-to-escort-daughter to college

14. See Ralph D. Russo. "Football coach moves game for daughter's wedding." Yahoo! Sports. Web. 12 September 2014. <http://sports.yahoo.com/news/fall-wedding-forces-football-coach-173945150--ncaaf.html>.

Simply compare the freedom of movement for white males with the restriction of decision for black males. Washington Redsk*ns receiver DeSean Jackson was criticized by sports media and fans for not attending off season workouts that were neither mandatory nor required. Joe Fortenbaugh. "Voluntary, Except." Yahoo! Sports. Web. 9 April, 2014. <http://sports.yahoo.com/news/voluntary-except-180050158--nfl.html>.

Chapter 6 References, pp. 72-82

1. In the late 1980s and early 1990s, Duke University fieled championship caliber basketball teams consistently. Duke was also criticized for consistently recruiting at that time, a consistent type of nonwhite player — one that challenged traditional notions of blackness. Such Duke players such as Grant Hill, Jay Williams, Shane Battier, Chris Duhon and others were then scrutinized for their representative "blackness." This issue has continued staying power, resulting in the New York Times publishing an open letter response by Grant Hill to former University of Michigan player Jalen Rose's comments about Hill's blackness nearly two decades after Rose and Hill played each other in college. See JRock. "V Exclusive: Grant Hill's Uncensored Open Letter Response To Jalen Rose." Vibe.com. Web. 17 March, 2011. <http://www. vibe.com/2011/03/v-exclusive-grant-hills-uncensored-open-letter-response-jalen-rose/>.

2. See endnote #17, Chapter 1. This explains the consistent production of narrative stories seldom seen elsewhere in white-dominated sports although possible that similar storylines exist such as the poor, unfortunate black boy who found love in the world through sport. One iteration of this narrative that captured the majority-white mainstream public's imagination was the blockbuster, Academy Award winning movie, "The Blind Side" based upon the award-winning book of the same name.

3. Consider how Pullman porter jobs were filled mostly by black males after the turn of the twentieth century who were expected to provide first-class, top rate service upon train cars to white patrons. Porters depended heavily upon tips and therefore appeared agreeable and obsequious. Additionally, founder George Pullman and management insisted that black porters provide service with a smile. To learn more, see: http://www.paulwagnerfilms.com/miles-of-smiles-about-porters/.

Even the infamous "Crying Jordan" meme is indicative of an once-awesome, one-man tour de force, being made "humble" (know your place) under the auspices of comic relief on mostly white fans' terms: http://www.nbcnewyork.com/news/sports/Crying-Jordan-Michael-Jordan-Meme-Ignites-the-Internet--374616681.html. It is worth considering why no notable, legendary, white male names in baseball (e.g., Cal Ripken, Jr.) have not fostered or generated nearly the amount of cult status even though Ripken "wiped away tears" whilst talking "about his family during his Hall of Fame induction speech in Cooperstown, N.Y." See < http://www.baltimoresun.com/sports/bal-bsripkeninduction3ox20070729143638-photo.html>.

4. See NFL Films: http://www.nfl.com/videos/nfl-films-presents/0ap2000000254372/NFL-Films-Presents-The-trash-talking-cornerback.

Additionally, see how Seattle Seahawks Sherman was directly juxtaposed against Model Citizen and hometown hero Champ Bailey of the Seahawks' Super Bowl opponent Denver Broncos in the lead up before the "big game." Whether a clever publicity stunt by a local company or not, telling is how in critiquing Sherman's infamous energetic interview with white female reporter Erin Andrews in the immediate aftermath of the National Football Conference championship game, the local appliance company felt the need to display a smiling, genteel Bailey as the antithesis of an "angry" Sherman. Romantic Racialism and Negrophobia strike again. See Anwar S. Richardon. "Denver appliance company takes a swing at Seahawks cornerback Richard Sherman." Yahoo! Sports. Web. 22 January 2014. <http://sports.yahoo.com/blogs/nfl-shutdown-corner/denver-appliance-company-takes-swing-seahawks-cornerback-richard-153057167--nfl.html>.

5. See Rachel Bertsche. "Celtic Rookie Buys Mom a House, Fulfills Childhood Promise." Yahoo! Parenting. Web. 4 November 2014. < https://www.yahoo.com/parenting/celtics-rookie-buys-mom-a-house-fulfills-childhood-101765151342.html>.

6. A familiar phrasing often emitted by black players in referencing their white coaches. See the transcript with player Michael Young referencing NCAA basketball head coach Jamie Dixon during the "March Madness" national tournament championship: "Press Conference: Pitt coach Jamie Dixon at ACC Tournament." Augusta Free Press. Web. 10 March, 2016. <http://augustafreepress.com/press-conference-pitt-coach-jamie-dixon-acc-tournament-2/>.

7. See endnote #3, Chapter 3.

8. See Andy Swift. "Tiger Woods Promises He'll Tell His Kids 'Face To Face' About His Infidelity!" Hollywood Life. Web. 19 November 2010. <http://hollywoodlife. com/2010/11/19/tiger-woods-cheating-kids-charlie-sam-elin-nordegren-interview/>.

Compare the condescending tone of moral superiority of the media clearly "knowing better" than Tiger in posing the query about how he will handle the intimate difficulty of addressing his children versus the resigned nature of merely wondering aloud why (white male) politicians cheat: CBS News. "Why Do Politicians Cheat?" Web. 25 June 2009. < http://www.cbsnews.com/news/why-do-politicians-cheat/>.

Lastly, also compare the media's tough journalistic stance about Tiger having to face the "tough questions" versus other high profile white athletes being "protected" from such intrusion: http://sports.yahoo.com/news/why-johnny-manziel-s-presence-has-browns-trying-to-block--hard-knocks-192348272.html

9. Fox Sports. "Wade-Stern Spat as NBA Talks Stall." Web. 1 October, 2011. < http:// www.foxsports.com/nba/story/Dwayne-Wade-shouts-at-David-Stern-as-NBA-talks-stall-in-New-York-100111>.

"The lockout illustrates the powerful ways that the black NBA player is conceptualized, imagined, and represented as a "'bad boy Black athlete" (Collins 2005, p. 153), defined by being "overly physical, out of control, prone to violence, driven by instinct, and hypersexual"; the white racial frame ubiquitously imagines NBA black ballers as "unruly and disrespectful," "inherently dangerous" and "in need of civilizing" (Ferber 2007, p. 20). Whether focusing on "intelligence," "levels of education," "maturity" and "disciplinarity," the NBA lockout discourse is a reminder of the powerful ways that the white "gaze" subjects blackness to "the prison of prior expectation" (Williams 1997, p. 74). Sarah Nilsen & Sarah E. Turner, eds. The Colorblind Screen: Television in Post-Racial America. New York: New York University Press, 2014.

It is fascinating to see mostly black NBA players branded as "selfish" during the NBA Lockout. If so, the players are self-absorbed and are not thinking about the best interests of who? White billionaire owners? Or upper middle class white fans who can afford direct access to such high quality live entertainment?

10. For additional material to independently investigate, consider these news stories about these nonwhite athletes and what they suggest about POWER & CONTROL:

>http://www.charlotteobserver.com/sports/nfl/carolina-panthers/nfl-blog/article34062744.html?ref=yfp

>http://sports.yahoo.com/news/rg3-forced-turn-religious-t-201301318.html

>http://www.sbnation.com/nfl/2015/2/13/8033117/an-open-letter-from-rg3s-future-child

>http://sports.yahoo.com/blogs/nba-ball-dont-lie/kevin-durant-nick-collison-kendrick-perkins-had-interesting-181918463--nba.html

Chapter 7 References, pp. 84-94

1. See Chapter 2, p. 30 with data culled from "The Status of Women in the U.S. Media 2014." Women's Media Center. Web. 2014. < http://wmc.3cdn. net/6dd3de8ca65852dbd4_fjm6yck9o.pdf>.

2. "Why We Love or Loath the Wide Receivers." The National. Web. 26 September, 2009. < http://www.thenational.ae/sport/north-american-sport/why-we-love-or-loath-the-wide-receivers>.

3. "Most white students find it reasonable to ask for '$50 million, or $1 million for each coming black year,' Hacker reports. 'And this calculation conveys, as well as anything, the value that white people place on their own skins. Indeed, to be white is to possess a gift whose value can be appreciated only after it is taken away. . . . The money would be used, as best it could, to buy protection from the discriminations and danger white people know they would face once they were perceived to be black.'" Clarence Petersen. "Two Nations: Black and White, Separate, Hostile, Unequal..." Chicago Tribune. Web. 26 February 1995. <http://articles.chicagotribune.com/1995-02-26/entertainment/9502260044_1_white-students-andrew-hacker-black>.

4. To learn more about the concept of "white privilege," attend the national White Privilege Conference or read up here: http://www.tolerance.org/article/racism-and-white-privilege.

5. Visit the website by Designer Skin to investigate the sale of "Smile! You're Darker" Maximum Bronzing Accelerator: http://www.designerskin.com/catalog/bronzer/smile-you-re-darker.

6. Various pictures of whites dressing up as blacks are never short in supply. While too numerous to list in detail here, a few, specific sports-related links to aid with your independent investigation of the truth are to follow. NOTE: some whites have taken the additional step, or gone the extra yard of donning "blackface," or an historically offensive gesture of appropriation dating back to America's minstrelsy era where whites would don burnt cork on their faces complete with extra large painted white or red lips and would portray black characters in demeaning and grossly exaggerated mannerisms:

> http://college.usatoday.com/2015/09/04/whitworth-soccer-players-suspended-from-game-for-wearing-blackface/

> http://www.usatoday.com/story/news/nation-now/2014/10/27/ray-rice-costume-domestic-violence/17994317/

> http://bustedcoverage.com/2011/10/28/73-spectacular-sports-halloween-costume-ideas-photos/mike-vick-blackface-halloween/

> http://www.foxsports.com/tennis/story/serena-williams-fans-wears-blackface-aussie-australian-open-final-twitter-explodes-013016

> http://www.theguardian.com/sport/2016/feb/21/liz-cambage-shocked-and-disturbed-after-opals-team-mate-dons-blackface

7. Observe the two stylized depictions of each athlete in these separate commercials; what do each suggest about the athletes's ability to interface with the poles of POWER & CONTROL?: Mike Trout: https://www.youtube.com/watch?v=0NQAqdYisME; Kevin Durant: https://www.youtube.com/watch?v=nEnejlZ2d54.

Chapter 8 References, pp. 96-106

1. Under the heading "First and 10: Physical Freaks," Derrius Guice is listed as number six: https://floridastate.rivals.com/content.asp?CID=1697066.

2. Players routinely strip down so potential employers can better inspect "the goods." Michael Silver. "Combine Meat Market a Little Disturbing." Yahoo! Sports. Web. 22 February 2008. < http://sports.yahoo.com/news/combine-meat-market-little-disturbing-075700491--nfl.html>.

3. "Gumbel Invokes Slavry in Stern Rant." Fox Sports. Web. 19 October, 2011. < http://www.foxsports.com/nba/story/HBO-Real-Sports-host-Bryant-Gumbel-invokes-slavery-in-rant-against-NBA-commissioner-David-Stern-101911>.

How can the horrors of the slave trade possibly be compared to a billion-dollar labor negotiation? Read more: http://www.newyorker.com/online/blogs/sportingscene/2011/10/economics-race-and-the-nba-lockout.html#ixzz1boYDtIPP.

Speaking of "slavery," consider this article on one athlete's association of this concept with sports: Yahoo! Sports. "Why Anthony Brown Called Steve Sarkisian A Racist." Web. 29 August, 2014. <https://sports.yahoo.com/news/why-anthony-brown-called-steve-140007228.html>.

4. Dan Devine. "D-League Players to Wear Devices that Measure, Track Heart Rate, Speed, Exertion, More during Games." Yahoo! Sports. Web. 14 February 2014. < http://sports.yahoo.com/blogs/nba-ball-dont-lie/d-league-players-to-start-wearing-devices-that-measure-and-track-heart-rate--speed--exertion--more-during-games-192915437.html>.

The technology, entitled OptimEye, is produced by Australian company Catapult Sports. Catapult's Gary McCoy further elaborates: "Imagine NASCAR, or even mechanically more precise, Formula 1 racing," McCoy said. "Powerful engines. High-performance mechanical needs. Could you imagine driving one of these vehicles without any dashboard whatsoever? What if you cant 'hear' the engine? Would you know when you are 'redlining,' causing untold overload to the system? The same happens every day for a high-powered NBA athlete — we drive them without a dashboard, we guess." Jeff Caplan. "Teams Advancing Fast at the Intersection of Science and Technology." NBA.com. Web. 17 August, 2013. < http://hangtime.blogs.nba.com/2013/08/17/teams-advancing-fast-at-the-intersection-of-science-and-technology/>.

Yet, problematic in McCoy's description is the objectification of the "NBA athlete" or black male athlete with the analogy that they are high performance vehicles driven without a dashboard; in other words these athletes, despite knowing all that they know about the game to play at an elite, professional level, still require guidance on how to be driven by white males who possess a self-proclaimed technological advantage.

Black athletes have also literally been commodified as stock in which individuals can invest. See Michael Liedtke. "Fantex IPO tied to 49er star wins fans in debut." Yahoo! Sports. Web. 28 April, 2014. <http://sports.yahoo.com/news/fantex-ipo-tied-49er-star-184513173--spt.html>.

5. Id.., "D-League Players to Wear Devices that Measure, Track Heart Rate, Speed, Exertion, More during Games."

6. In 2011, Pittsburgh Pirates pitcher Ross Ohlendorf won his arbitration case and received a raise of 361% to $2.025M annually despite being paid $439,000 the year before and having a win-loss record of 1-11 (meaning one win and eleven losses). Rob Biertempfel. "Arbitrators: Pirates Will Pay 1-11 Pitcher $2 Million This Year." TribLive.com [The Pittsburgh and Westmoreland Tribune-Review]. Web. 10 February, 2011.   <http://triblive.com/mobile/1954626-81/strong-million-ohlendorf-pirates-arbitration-1-11-player-record-ross-salary>.

7. Eric Freeman. "NBA to track 'hustle stats' at Vegas Summer League for teams, fans." Yahoo! Sports. Web. 9 July 2015. http://sports.yahoo.com/blogs/nba-ball-dont-lie/nba-to-track--hustle-stats--at-vegas-summer-league-for-teams--fans-235828503.html

8. Joe Kay. "NFL Network Apologizes to Bengals Shown Naked on TV." Yahoo! Sports. Web. 19 October, 2015. <http://sports.yahoo.com/news/nfl-network-apologizes-bengals-shown-naked-tv-205027588--nfl.html>.

9. Taylor Branch. "The Shame of College Sports." The Atlantic. Web. October 2011. < http://www.theatlantic.com/magazine/archive/2011/10/the-shame-of-college-sports/308643/ >. It must be noted that while definitely direct, such comments were said AFTER Brown retired; white privilege suggests that Brown can "afford" to be controversial since little can be done to punish an older, rich, retired white male.

10. For an example of an endowed and empowered white male within the sports world, look no further than NFL Commissioner Roger Goodell. Notwithstanding his "work ethic," to say the least, this individual was born into a life of privilege. Consider the opening paragraph of the following article cited: "Roger Goodell always looked the part: tall and handsome, with the perfect blond locks and the expensive tailored suits. This guy, no doubt, casts a presence. He was trained for power, the son of a U.S. senator, raised in Westchester County affluence, joining the NFL offices right out of college with upward mobility as the end game." See Dan Wetzel. "The hell of Roger Goodell: Tarnishing the shield and mudslinging with TMZ." Yahoo! Sports. 9 September, 2014.

11. In this picture taken for Vogue magazine, NFL New York Giants wide receiver Victor Cruz is depicted with supermodel Kate Upton. Both individuals are known for their "body of work." based upon their bodies. Yet, in this depiction, Cruz is shirtless holding his uniform reminding the viewer that all he is a football player with defined abdominal muscles, while Upton appears to be "normal" in a modest sundress, although part of her celebrity is staked upon her typically glamorized in more revealing states of dress. The title of the article only underscores the physical fascination/objectification of Cruz/presence, at least in this photograph. Swoonworthy. "Victor Cruz and His Abs Pose With Kate Upton for Vogue." Web. 29 January, 2014. <http://swoonworthy.net/victor-cruz-abs-pose-kate-upton-vogue/>.

Chapter 9 References, pp. 108-118

1. Links to the examples refernced include:

Sean Payton: http://espn.go.com/nfl/story/_/id/7718136/sean-payton-new-orleans-saints-banned-one-year-bounties.

Steve Masiello: http://www.si.com/college-basketball/2015/03/13/steve-masiello-manhattan-resume-scandal-si-now.

Dave Bliss: https://www.yahoo.com/sports/blogs/ncaab-the-dagger/dave-bliss-returns-to-college-coaching-12-years-after-baylor-scandal-222949418.html.

Bobby Petrino: http://sports.yahoo.com/news/why-louisville-fans-embrace-bobby-petrino-when-nobody-else-will-060113487-ncaaf.html.

Rick Pitino: http://espn.go.com/mens-college-basketball/news/story?id=4392828.

2. See Chapter 6, Model Citizen Example #10. Is Cam Newton dabbing the problem or is Cam Newton the problem? http://www.sbnation.com/lookit/2016/1/19/10791740/tennis-video-australian-open-victoria-azarenka-dab; http://thesource.com/2016/03/21/victoria-azarenka-beats-serena-dabs-on-her-at-indian-wells/.

Further compare the pressure upon black males to emulate Model behavior with white athletes (e.g., Johnny Manziel) who are flagrant in their disregard of rules, policies and structures:

>http://www.theroot.com/articles/news/2016/02/report_johnny_manziel_struck_ex_girlfriend_several_times_during_argument.html?wpisrc=see_also_article

>http://sports.yahoo.com/news/manziel-dont-think-im-doing-151928215--nfl.html

>http://espn.go.com/nfl/story/_/id/14801904/dallas-police-acquire-colleen-crowley-medical-records-johnny-manziel-case

>https://sports.yahoo.com/news/surprising-move-johnny-manziel-not-222514092.html

>https://www.yahoo.com/sports/news/why-johnny-manziel-better-risk-145600458.html

>http://profootballtalk.nbcsports.com/2014/07/07/manziels-latest-vegas-trip-creates-an-interesting-photo/#comments

>https://sports.yahoo.com/news/manziel-becomes-johnny-jamboogie-snickers-191118613--nfl.html

>http://www.sbnation.com/lookit/2014/8/28/6080801/johnny-manziel-roger-staubach-are-bad-roommates-in-new-ad

3. 2015 Silverado commercial: https://www.youtube.com/watch?v=9nxC1zsQTVk.

Chapter 10 References, pp. 120-130

1. See endnote #4, Chapter 5.

2. Donald H. Yee. "College Sports Exploits Unpaid Black Athletes. But They Could Force a Change." The Washington Post. Web. 8 January, 2016. < https://www. washingtonpost.com/posteverything/wp/2016/01/08/college-sports-exploits-unpaid-black-athletes-but-they-could-force-a-change/>.

College athletics is essentially a quasi-professional league although the NCAA enjoys non-profit status. Although they care about players and the integrity of the game, many white male head coaches of basketball and football D-I programs earn millions annually and spend hundreds of thousands of dollars on functions in which they deem important (http://m.thepostgame.com/blog/dish/201501/kentucky-basketball-dropped-800000-lavish-trip-bahamas).

3. Compare the current, sleek footage of the NBA to what Dr. Naismith describes as his original idea through this 1939 radio interview: https://www.youtube.com/watch?v=ESViBLNs_y8.

4. Larry Johnson, Albert Haynesworth, Warren Sapp, Rashard Mendenhall, Adrian Peterson (http://newyork.cbslocal.com/2014/04/28/in-wake-of-sterling-fiasco-ex-knicks-great-larry-johnson-appears-to-call-for-all-black-league/).

5. Every MLB player wears the number "42" in Jackie Robinson's honor: http://m.mlb.com/news/article/118578184/teams-across-mlb-honor-jackie-robinsons-impact-on-special-day.

6. "Ferry Steps Down as Hawks GM after Racist Remarks." Yahoo! Sports. Web. 22 June 2015. < http://sports.yahoo.com/news/ferry-steps-down-hawks-gm-racist-remarks-172942681--nba.html>.

Recall, Ferry made these comments during a "private" conversation. In what Dr. Joe Feagin labels as "Front Stage, Back Stage" behavior, Ferry would be less inclined to speak offensively when in the presence of blacks although he may still harbor problematic thoughts.

7. Ralph Miller. "The NCAA Exploits the College Athletes for whom You Love to Root." The Guardian. Web. 3 September, 2015. < http://www.theguardian.com/commentisfree/2015/sep/03/the-ncaa-exploits-the-college-athletes-for-whom-you-love-to-root>.

8. The University of Chicago conducted a study entitled "Are Emily and Brendan More Employable than Lakisha and Jamal?" with the finding that white-sounding names are 50% more likely to get called back for an initial interview than identical applicants with black sounding names. Erza Klein. "Racism Isn't Over. But Policymakers from both Parties Like to Pretend It Is." The Washington Post. Web. 1 December 2013. < https://www.washingtonpost.com/news/wonk/wp/2013/12/01/racism-isnt-over-but-policymakers-from-both-parties-like-to-pretend-it-is/>.

9. See below; see what else you can find online:

>http://www.theroot.com/articles/culture/2014/03/racism_in_high_school_sports_
has_deeper_causes.html

>https://www.youtube.com/watch?v=TVjbYFqhAfM

>http://mic.com/articles/137591/high-school-officials-apologize-after-ignoring-
racist-chants-at-a-basketball-game#.tC50QrOKy

>http://www.theguardian.com/world/2012/mar/30/black-power-salute-1968-olympics

>http://sports.yahoo.com/blogs/nfl-shutdown-corner/terrell-owens-suggests-
racism-reason-different-reactions-dez-185521685--nfl.html

10. See: >http://sports.yahoo.com/blogs/mlb-big-league-stew/banana-tossing-
giants-fan-says-gesture-wasn-t-001648859.html

>http://espn.go.com/nhl/story/_/id/7007219/fan-throws-banana-philadelphia-
flyers-winger-wayne-simmonds

11. Similarly, trailblazer Jackie Robinson, while honored and respected now,
posthumously, entitled his autobiography, "I Never Had it Made." See Larry Schwartz.
"Owens Pierced a Myth." ESPN.com. Web. N.d. < https://espn.go.com/sportscentury/
features/00016393.html>.

12. Eric Edholm. "T.O. Suggests Racism is Reason for Different Reactions to Dez
Bryant, Tom Brady Sideline Blowups." Yahoo! Sports. Web. 29 October, 2013. < http://
sports.yahoo.com/blogs/nfl-shutdown-corner/terrell-owens-suggests-racism-reason-
different-reactions-dez-185521685--nfl.html>.

13. For background on two of MLB's more famous "legends," see Mark Newman.
"Curses! Cubs Haunted by History." MLB.com. Web. 5 October, 2007. <http://mlb.mlb.
com/news/print.jsp?ymd=20071005&content_id=2251172&c_id=mlb>.

About the Author

Frederick Gooding, Jr. is an Associate Professor
in *Texas Christian University's* Honors College
who continues to travel the world in pursuit of his
independent investigation of the truth.

www.theracedoc.com

FOR MORE INFORMATION

For more information about racial analysis within mainstream
media and other product offerings from
On the Reelz Press visit us online at:

www.otrpress.com

On the Reelz
PRESS

Thank you for reading *You Mean, There's RACE in My Sports?*
May you never see mainstream sports the same way again . . .

CPSIA information can be obtained
at www.ICGtesting.com
Printed in the USA
LVHW030639300821
696398LV00011B/1261